Tagore's *Chitra* and Aurobindo's *Savitri*

A Comparative Study

KETKI N. PANDYA

Published by
ATLANTIC PUBLISHERS AND DISTRIBUTORS
B-2, Vishal Enclave, Opp. Rajouri Garden, New Delhi-110027
Phones : 25413460, 25429987, 25466842

Sales Office
7/22, Ansari Road, Darya Ganj, New Delhi-110002
Phones : 23273880, 23275880, 23280451
Fax : 91-11-23285873
web : www.atlanticbooks.com
e-mail : info@atlanticbooks.com

ISBN 81-269-0353-8

Printed in India at
Nice Printing Press, Delhi

DEDICATED TO

My Dear Father
(Late) Dr. Naresh Balvantray Pandya

Who loved and cared for me

And

My Dear Mother
Smt. Smita Pandya

Who still continues to inspire me

Preface

The book *Tagore's Chitra and Aurobindo's Savitri: A Comparative Study* offers a novel reading of the *Chitra* and *Savitri* legends. The study not only documents the contemporary socio-cultural, religious, political and literary conditions of the times but also comparatively analyses the content, form and philosophy of *Chitra* and *Savitri*. A number of ideas that eventually emerge revolve on self-analysis, self-evolution, self-awakening, self-knowledge and self-transcendence. In effect, the core idea of the two works is the *anubhuti* (experience) of self-realization or the attainment of *Vidya* (knowledge) which perhaps can be better understood now in the light of the woman condition that *knows* how to subvert the male strategies of domination. Thus, the reformist ideology of Tagore and Aurobindo continues to have a contextual relevance and appeal.

I take this opportunity to express my sense of gratitude to several persons who have helped me in the writing of this book. My sincere thanks are due to Dr. Avadhesh Kumar Singh, my esteemed guide and Head of the Department of English and Comparative Literary Studies, Saurashtra University, Rajkot for his able guidance and systematic criticism during the course of the present study. I am indebted to him for the many privileges and boundless compassion showered upon me throughout the tenure of my research. I run short of words to express my feelings of gratitude for him.

I owe my heart-felt gratitude to my mother Smt. Smita Pandya for having continuously inspired me throughout my period of study and remember my father (Late) Dr. Naresh Balvantray Pandya with fondness on this occasion.

I am also thankful to my mother-in-law (Late) Smt. Pramila Nagar and my father-in-law Dr. Rama Shanker Nagar for having encouraged me on all fronts.

My thanks are due to my husband Dr. Anupam Nagar who not only helped me by going through the book but also motivated me incontinently.

I am profoundly indebted to Shri Devendra Acharya, Principal, Gurukul Mahila College, Porbandar for encouraging and extending all the library facilities to me from time to time.

I owe my gratitude to Dr. Harin Majithia, Head, Department of English, Gurukul Mahila College, Porbandar for her critical suggestions, sharing her literary and critical materials and extending moral support during the course of my study.

Thanks are also due to Dhavala, Poorvi and Preetida Pandya, my sisters, Vasundhara and Mamta, my sisters-in-law, Vinayak and Padamnabhi Nagar, my brothers-in-law for their priceless assistance.

My thanks are also due to all those who unmentioned though they are, yet were of invaluable help in one way or the other.

KETKI NARESHPRASAD PANDYA

CONTENTS

1

TAGORE'S *CHITRA* AND AUROBINDO'S *SAVITRI*: A STUDY IN BACKGROUND

1. INTRODUCTION

Rabindranath Tagore's drama *Chitra* reminds man that the ultimate truth is to be found not at the physical level but in the steady evolution of the self. The illumination of a young princess' mind lies in the recognition and realization that it is in Truth alone that true happiness resides. Similarly Aurobindo's epic *Savitri* narrates the story of a young princess who saves the life of her husband from Death and thereby suggests the ultimate liberation of man from universal Death. Aurobindo, therefore, writes poetry to enunciate his philosophy in terms of spiritual action and vision. *Chitra* and *Savitri* are Upanishadic works in the sense that their principal theme is the search for *vidya* (knowledge), that liberates man from *avidya* (ignorance), and that their main stylistic device is the conversation between the human and divine characters.

Evolution is the watchword of both Tagore and Aurobindo. The awakening of the self or raising the life and existence to a higher level of consciousness is one of the parallel themes observed in *Chitra* and *Savitri*. Further, the integral transformation of *Chitra* and *Savitri* and their inner intuitive development has a much wider connotation to mankind at large. An endeavour is made to establish *Chitra* and *Savitri* as works of self-discovery. Although there are fundamental differences in terms of the nature of Chitra and Savitri's awareness, yet there is no denying that these legends from the *Mahabharata* are exquisite examples of the female aspect of the Indian Women.

Tagore and Aurobindo primarily seek to achieve a realization of human unity, universal peace and happiness, based on a spiritual foundation, which ensure the orderly progress and fulfilment of human destiny. *Chitra* and *Savitri* are concerned with the consciousness of Man and how it, like all other living things, grows according to its own nature. The play and the epic offer to mankind the spectacle of a rebirth of life in spiritual terms. The heroines of *Chitra* and *Savitri* extend their consciousness by their experiences of life and eventually acquire self-knowledge and self-transcendence. They educate themselves in the self by seeing themselves, their false selves, and finally their whole transcendental beings. The action in both the works is internal, manifesting an uplifting of thought, feeling and sense. The inner mind is the focal point of the two works. They also bear witness to self-expansion and the conscious subjectivity of the modern feminine mind. Their inwardness is intolerant of asceticism of religion on the one hand and the abstraction of philosophy on the other. They rather meditate on the truth of life and the truth of the spirit respectively.

However, in order to have an exact idea about the purpose of understanding *Chitra* and *Savitri*, it is essential to familiarize oneself with the background in terms of the age of Indian Renaissance in which Rabindranath Tagore and Aurobindo Ghose lived. The study of the social, cultural, religious, political, economical and literary conditions of the Indian Renaissance that had a profound impact in shaping the mind and spirit of Tagore and Aurobindo becomes important in order to grasp the chief tenets of their philosophy and literary acumen. Further, a brief survey of Indian English Poetry is attempted to put the poets in proper view. Next, the literary output of the two poets is outlined to place *Chitra* and *Savitri* in perspective. And finally the objectives of the present study are stated.

1.1 The Indian Renaissance

Rabindranath Tagore and Aurobindo Ghose were not only the products of the Indian Renaissance but also active participants in it. They sprang up when the old order was wearing out and the new was emerging forth; when the people were looking for new thoughts and ideals. Social revolutions, cultural changes, and religious and political movements sweeping different parts of the country marked the Indian Renaissance. The purpose of all these movements was to seek social reformation and the independence of India.

Though the Indian Renaissance was only explicitly seen in the nineteenth century, it implicitly had already started a century earlier. The British East India Company had defeated Nawab Siraj-ud-Daulah in the battle of Plassey in June 1757 A.D.[1] Secondly, the Mughal emperor Shah Alam II was defeated in 1764 in the battle of Buxar and in 1765, he gave the Diwani of Bengal, Bihar and Orissa to the English East India Company.[2] The Britishers also defeated the other two powerful communities *i.e.*, the Marathas and the Sikhs. The unity of the Marathas was destroyed due to their internal enmity and conflict. They got defeated in the wars of Asi (1803) and Lasvari (1803). The Britishers also defeated the Sikhs in 1849. In 1856, Awadh was also included in the British Empire. In this way, the whole country was brought under control and was ruled over by the Britishers,[3] but the inhumanity, cruelty and hard-hearted attitude of the Britishers brought about dissatisfaction and disappointment among the countrymen. Consequently, they got united and rebelled against the British Rule in 1857.

The struggle of 1857 was historically significant, as it had shaken the foundations of British imperialism in India. Actually the conditions of rebellion had been taking shape for the last many years. A small beginning turned into a countrywide struggle. However this brought about the end of the East India Company's rule in India and thereafter the colony of India came directly under Queen Victoria's rule.[4] Another important result of the 1857 mutiny was that for the first time the Indians became conscious of the British rule. The later nineteenth century in particular witnessed a complete revolutionary change in every aspect of Indian life. The new education system, the establishment of the printing industry, the railway network, the post and telegraphs department threw rays of western life and culture on the Indian soil. And this hastened the arrival of the Indian Renaissance.

The Indian Renaissance played a vital role in the formation of the nineteenth century Indian mind and cast its shadow on the twentieth century Indian intellectual and creative pursuits. The Indian Renaissance that took place in the nineteenth century was unlike the Western Renaissance that was witnessed in the fifteenth and sixteenth centuries. Though the commonly used expression for the Indian Renaissance is 'Punarjagaran-Kal' or 'Navjagaran-Kal,'[5-6-7] for the sake of convenience the term Indian Renaissance would be employed in the present study.

1.1.1 *Social, Cultural and Religious Conditions of the Indian Renaissance*

The Indian encounter with the western civilization was a historical accident that shook the Indian people. This resulted in the awakening and modernization of the society but this change was not in agreement with the old religious traditions, human values and classes. Therefore a necessity for synthesis was highly felt between the present day requirements and the old conventions. At this juncture a small but lively class, in India and particularly in Bengal and Maharashtra, which was tormented by an unprecedented cultural encounter, emerged. This group of Indian thinkers and reformers was extremely conscious of external cultural, religious, economic and political exploitation. What should be accepted and what should be rejected? What should be preserved and what should be thrown off?—were the questions plaguing the minds of the Indian thinkers and reformers in that age of transition. This enlightened minority tried to awaken the majority of the people oblivious of this crisis. Tagore, Aurobindo, Ram Mohan Roy, Vivekananda, Gandhi, Nehru, Lal-Bal-Pal and other patriots had voiced this dilemma for their generation. These thinkers, writers and founders of the different societies *i.e.,* Brahmo Samaj, Prarthana Samaj, Theosophy Society, Arya Samaj, Sanatana Dharma and Vedanta Darshan, were the most important and most effective instruments in ushering forward the Indian Renaissance. These movements tried to resist and respond to this process of transition in their own way as per their ideology, attitude, ambience and predilections. Even during the middle-ages the Bhakti Andolan had begun against casteism, untouchability, vanity and hypocrisy. The synthesis then brought about was emotional in nature but during the Indian Renaissance the amalgamation brought about was based on logic and discrimination. Therefore the ideology of almost all the varied schools of thought during the nineteenth century was primarily reason-oriented.

The reason-oriented school included Raja Ram Mohan Roy and his followers. According to him modern Europe was a creation of the Renaissance which had begun with Francis Bacon's *New Organum*. For the redemption of Indian culture, for bringing about necessary changes to meet challenges in future and for material and spiritual progress it was considered necessary to accept and assimilate the western scientific attitude. The religious and social movement initiated by Raja Ram Mohan Roy had greatly energized the Indian people.

Raja Ram Mohan Roy founded the 'Brahmo Samaj' in 1828. He was well versed in Arabic and Persian and made himself acquainted with the Greek thinkers such as Socrates, Plato and Aristotle through Arabic translations. He studied the *Bhagavad Gita* and the Upanishads. He took the help of the Upanishads in order to protest against superstitions and idol worship. Brahmo Samaj attacked various social evils under his leadership. He was an intelligent social reformer. According to him, caste system was inhuman and anti-national. He would be remembered forever for his effort to protest against the *sati*-system. He was in favour of widow re-marriage and voiced for the equal rights of men and women.[8] The Samaj received a forceful stimulus at the hands of Devendranath Tagore, the 'Maharshi.' He gave it a new direction, when the movement was whimpering out. His intention was to put an end to the limitations and traditions of the time. For Hinduism, he went to the Vedas and the Upanishads. The Brahmo Samaj thus was a power in Bengal, the meeting point of both the religious and the cultural Renaissance.

Rajnarain Bose, the maternal grandfather of Aurobindo also asserted that the Brahmo Dharma, which embodied the essence of the original Hinduism of Vedanta, was not only superior to Christianity but was in fact the key to the science of religion. The Brahmo Samaj played a vital role in bringing about social reforms and political awareness in the Indian Movement for Independence. It initiated activities that gave momentum to ideas pertaining to political freedom and self-determination.

Mahadev Govind Ranade worked for the spread of social reforms and education and founded the Prarthana Samaj in 1867 in Maharashtra. He was the founder and motivating force of the national social conference. His Prarthana-Samaj aimed at stemming the tide of Hindu-decadence caused by ritualism, orthodoxy, and skepticism verging on cynicism produced by the influence of the western thoughts. Ranade was the most intelligent person of the nineteenth century India.[9] He thought logically over all the religious and social problems. He continuously emphasized on the equality of human beings. He did not favour casteism but was in favour of inter-caste marriages and women education. He tried to mould Indian culture in accordance with new scientific ideology.[10]

Swami Sahjanand, born in a small village Chhapaiya near Ayodhya of United Province, came to Gujarat in 1801 and founded the Swaminarayan sect. He strove to reform the Gujarati society infested with religious orthodoxy and ignorance, poverty and the harmful living style of the backward classes of the society. He influenced the average people by his moral ideology and value-based behaviour.[11]

Dayanand Saraswati, born in Tankara village of Saurashtra, established the Arya Samaj in Bombay in 1867. His Arya Samaj was based on strict orthodox Hinduism whereas the Brahmo Samaj was more receptive and assimilative. Dayanand, well versed in Sanskrit, expressed his arguments logically in *Satyarth Prakash*. For him, the Vedas were the basis for Arya Samaj. According to him, Vedic religion was the only truth.[12] There was no place for class divisions and inequality between man and man and between men and women. His was really a democratic vision. He believed that western education was necessary for material progress. He founded the Dayanand Anglo-Vedic College in 1886. Arya Samaj made a distinctive contribution to carry national ideology.[13] Gujarat, Uttar Pradesh, Haryana, Rajasthan and Punjab were much influenced by Arya Samaj. This movement strongly attacked untouchability, astrology and advocated vegetarianism.

Many other social institutions also came into existence that aimed at social reformation and encouragement of people's aptitude for imbibing the Indian culture. Annie Beasant awakened the nationality of the country through the Theosophical Society. Madam Blavatsky and Cl. Olkat established the Theosophical Society in New York in 1875. One of its branches was set up in Adyar (Madras) in 1882. Annie Beasant joined the English branch in 1888. She came to India in 1893 and devoted her life for the works of this society. She delivered lectures in favour of Indian spirituality. She also opened educational institutions like the Central Hindu College in Baneras.

Ishwar Chandra Vidyasagar became the most determined social reformer after Ram Mohan Roy. Likewise, the task of religious regeneration was taken up by Keshav Chandra Sen. Kashinath Telang was deeply read in English and Sanskrit and he translated the *Bhagavat Geeta* for the sacred books of the East Series. The climate of the time was so intellectually and morally invigorating that it brought into existence institutions like the Paramhansa Sabha that laid emphasis on the pure worship of God. Gopal Krishna Gokhale and Sir Narayan Chandavarkar's contribution is also worth noting.

Ramkrishna Paramhansa arrived at the nick of time, so modern India, then, had the spiritual Messiah she needed to save Indian culture and set it on new foundations. He, together with his disciple Vivekananda stressed upon the need of nationality and threw light on the real form of *Dharma.* Vivekananda established the Ramakrishna Mission, a spiritual and humanitarian movement after the death of Ramkrishna Paramhansa in 1897. He went to Chicago to represent India in the Parliament of World-Religions in 1893. His eloquence impressed one and all. Coming back to India, he opposed caste-system, untouchability. He made the Indians realize that the culture of India was incomparable in its excellence. He attracted our attention to equality, unity, brotherhood, and independence.[14]

Mohandas Karamchand Gandhi was also born during the Indian Renaissance. His philosophy was based on the *Bhagavad Geeta's* 'Anasakti Yoga.' Satya and Ahimsa were the strong weapons with the help of which he changed his dreams into reality.

Thus, a new climate, relying on the positive aspects of the ideas of Raja Rammohan Roy, Devendranath Tagore, Rajnarain Bose, Ranade, Dayanand Saraswati, and Annie Beasant, came into existence due to which India was seen as a nation with rich cultural and spiritual heritage.

Among those whose views concentrated on reforming Hindu religion, Vivekananda was one of the foremost and far-reaching voices. A seer possessed with modern thinking, he was a sanyasin with a scientific bent of mind but not an orthodox Vedantist. He stressed liberal humanitarian Hindu religion and opposing fanatic subscription to superstitions and dogmatism, he wanted to extricate the society from the cruel, parasitic clutches of priesthood and ritualism and then assimilate the elements of modern science and civilization. With full reverence to original thoughts of the predecessors, he did not oversight the role of the west in the Indian Renaissance. He criticized the ills of the western capitalistic system. He voiced his anger against prevailing orthodoxy in the Indian society. Meanwhile, in India there was a tremendous revival of religion. He was proud to belong to India that sheltered the persecuted, the refugees of all religions and nations of the world. The mantra of Vivekananda was to be broad and sincere in our understanding of equality for the realization of human civilization.

The Indian Renaissance greatly influenced Rabindranath and Aurobindo too. Rabindranath's humanistic viewpoint had been profoundly influenced by Paramahansa, Vivekananda, Annie Beasant and Raja Ram Mohan Roy. According to Tagore, both Japan and India had to guard themselves against the temptation to ape the West in the name of modernization; for true modernization is freedom of the mind. For Tagore, the real problem of India was not political but social. He wanted our civilization to take a firm stand upon its basis of social co-operation and not upon that of economic exploitation and conflict. He played an important part in the history of the Indian Renaissance. His father encouraged him to study the Upanishads. He left no stone unturned to check the wave of conversion to Christianity in Bengal. Tagore also became the secretary of the Adi Brahmo Samaj of which his father was one of the greatest advocates. He was a nationalist and developed a critical attitude to the evils in the Hindu society. Bengal saw a great political and social upheaval on account of the Swadeshi movement in 1905, which resulted in the protest against the partition of Bengal by Lord Curzon. It soon climaxed into a strong agitation in India for the attainment of Independence. Tagore lectured in meetings and organized processions. He considered that Swaraj was not a boon to be begged but it was a right to be obtained.

Aurobindo was a revolutionary political leader and was much influenced by the ideology of Ramakrishna Paramhansa. He was a true patriot. It was C.R. Das, later the celebrated 'Deshbandhu' Chittaranjan, who described Aurobindo as the poet of patriotism, the prophet of nationalism and the lover of humanity.[15] He believed that the country was the Mother and declared with disarming frankness that complete independence was the goal of India's national awakening. This had a thrilling impact on the mind of young India. He gave a call for the boycott of foreign goods.[16] He was against caste system. His creative works reveal his experience of spiritual bliss. His 'Ati-Manavvad' emphasizes on the aspiration of bringing Heaven upon the earth. The motto of Vivekananda's true successor, Aurobindo, was self-realization. For him the Indian Renaissance was a thing of mental development, which was concerned with spiritual integration and self-realization. According to him, the Indian Renaissance was a new creation of the Indian Swadharma. However, he did not negate the western influence but stressed upon the self-creative aspect of the Indian Renaissance. As a thinker he tried to understand it in dialectical terms. In the first phase he saw the enthusiastic reception of the European encounter and the revolutionary rejection of the principles of the ancient Indian culture. In the second phase he marked the forceful resistance and rejection of everything western, along with preservation of everything native. And in the third phase he observed the synthesis that creatively transformed and Indianized everything in the process.

Durgaram Mehtaji, Dalpatram, Narmad also endeavoured to encourage the people of India. They were Gujarati poets but mainly they were social reformers. In Gujarat, Durgaramji founded 'Manavdharma Sabha' and protested against inequality, compulsory widowhood, superstitions, idol-worship and other evils of the time. Dalpatram was a patriot. He was appointed as secretary of the Gujarat Vernacular Society in 1847. He was the editor of the magazine *Buddhiprakash*. He advised his countrymen to protest against the social evils like child marriage and abortion. Concentrating on the problem of widow re-marriage, he wrote *Vencharitra* in 1868. He wrote to irradiate the prevailing superstitions and wrong social traditions. Narmad delivered lectures and wrote articles regarding reformation under the name of 'Buddhivardhak Sabha.' Mahipatram founded 'Prarthana Sabha' in Gujarat. His intention was to worship the formless God.[17]

'Shreya-Sadhak Adhikari Varg' was an institute founded by Nrusinhacharya in Baroda in the last decade of the nineteenth century. Nathuram Sharma, Upendracharya and Chhotalal Jivanlal Master 'Vishva-Vandya' strove to enliven the tradition of Hindu religion and rituals. They also published a magazine titled as *Mahakal* from Baroda.

The Hindi poets of the Indian Renaissance also threw light on the conditions responsible for upliftment or degradation of their motherland and thereby sowed the seeds of nationality in the Indian mind. Bhartendu's *Vijayinee Vijay Vaijayanti*, Premdhan's *Anand Arunoday*, Pratapnarayan Mishra's *Mahaparva* and *Naya Samvat* and Radhakrishnadas's *Bharat Barahmasa* and *Vinay* are the poems infused with patriotism. They gave the message of national reawakening and reformation. Bhartendu wrote a play *Bharat Durdasha* depicting the narrow meaning of the caste system. In *Man Ki Laher*, Pratapnarayan Mishra observed the miserable condition of child widows. Balkrishna Bhatt's *Nai Roshni Ka Vish*, Devakinandan Tripathi's *Bharat-Haran* are some other significant plays showing the prevailing situation of India. These playwrights wished to awaken the mind of the people and create self-confidence in them. Radhakrishnadas's *Nissahay Hindu*, Srinivasdas's *Pariksha Guru*, Balkrishna Bhatt's *Nutan Brahmachari* are the novels that protest against the social evils of the time and give the message of the ideal family and society.

Thus, Religion meant much to all these Indian Renaissance thinkers and writers. It was not just coincidental but was rooted in that aspect of Indian psyche, which considered religion to be the integrating force. Contrary to the extreme individualism of the west, society (religion, culture and country) was in the centre of concerns for all leaders of the Indian Renaissance. The social thinkers recognized religion to be the rock bottom of Indian society and so founded their model for social reforms on religion.

Briefly speaking, when India was under the British rule, she was exploited in the field of politics and economics but on the other hand, new life can be observed in the social, religious and cultural conditions of the time. All these movements, institutions and reformers helped in the irradiation of wrong conceptions, traditions and superstitions. The downtrodden, the exploited ones and women were sympathized. In short, the age was remarkable for its Humanism and Spiritualism.

1.1.2. *Political Conditions of the Indian Renaissance*

The Indian Renaissance included many events as, the establishment of the British East India Company, the sepoy's mutiny, the establishment of the Victorian Empire in India, the foundation of the Indian National Congress, the Bang-Bhang Movement, the First World War, the Minto Morley Reforms, the Rowlatt Act, the Jaliyanwalla Baug Massacre, the Khilafat Andolan, the Non-cooperation Movement of Gandhiji, the establishment of Swarajya Party, the separation of Jinnah from the Congress and the unification with the Muslim League Unity brought about by various meetings and committees between the Congress and the Government, the Election in 1936-37 and the establishment of the Mantri-Mandal of the Congress and other parties, the beginning of the Second World War, the resignation of the Congress Ministry in 1939, the demand for Pakistan in 1940, the visit of Lord Cripps to India, the Quit India Movement in 1942, the establishment of the Interim Government in 1946, the communal fights in Calcutta, Noakhali, Bihar and Punjab due to the scornful policy of the Muslim League, the Independence of India on 15th of August, 1947 and many other issues of the country.

The Britishers won Bengal in 1757 and Delhi in 1857. In between they spread their power in other parts of India. They followed their own Ruling and Financial Policy. In order to facilitate their own political work, they started schools and colleges so that they could get Indian clerks. The beginning of the Printing Press in India and Lord Dalhousie's Policy were the main incidents of this period. The result was that Satara, Jhansi, Nagpur, Jetpur (M.P.) were merged into the British Empire which affected the country socially, financially, literally as well as politically.

Following the mutiny of 1857 it was clear to the Indians that the Britishers had been ruling by adopting the policy of divide and rule. Gradually, rulers like Nana Saheb and his secretary Ajmulla spread over the ideology of freedom in various states of India against the British rule. It was on 9th May 1857 when the fire of anger against the Britishers broke out. It continued for the whole year. Nana Saheb, Ahmed Shah, Tatiya Tope and the Queen of Jhansi and other brave soldiers strove to achieve their goal. However, the rebellion was a failure due to the diplomacy of the British army and the treachery of the Indian kings. Later the effect of the Victorian regime was sighted in India. The policy of religious tolerance came into force. Lord Macaulay's propaganda regarding the supremacy of the English culture, language and literature was observed. These factors led to changes in the Indian society as a result of politics, which was indirect and dirty at the same time.

In 1866, Rajnarain Bose published a prospectus for a 'Society for the promotion of National Feeling among the Educated Natives of Bengal.'[18] An annual 'Jatiya Mela' or National Gathering, patterned after ideas in Rajnarain's prospectus, became so popular that it was given a permanent form in the 'Jatiya Sabha' or the National Society. This organization was a harbinger of the movements of the 1870s that culminated in the foundation of the Indian National Congress.

Around this time a number of amateur Secret Societies sprang up in Calcutta; Rajnarain headed one of them, of which the young Rabindranath Tagore was a member. He was a forerunner in both the political and the revolutionary movements. That was the reason why Rajnarain Bose was looked on as a modern rishi and had received the affectionate title, by which he is still remembered—the Grandfather of Indian Nationalism.

In 1885, the Indian National Congress was established which aimed at assisting and improving the governance of the Indian administration. But with the entry of Bal Gangadhar Tilak, the Congress changed its ideology with the sole aim of fighting for complete independence. The Bang-Bhang law had strengthened the earning for Indian independence and the revolutionary institutions had been established internally and developed in order to bring an end to the British rule. The important names who actively participated in these institutions were Tilak, Hardayal, Aurobindo Ghose, Ras Bihari Bose, Surendranath Banerjee, Sachindranath, Bhagat Singh, Chandrashekhar Azad, Sukhdev and Rajguru. The First World War started in 1914 and was over in 1919. The Indians were all the more disappointed due to the Rowlatt Act and the Jaliyanwalla Baug Massacre.

In 1920, Gandhiji took over the leadership of the Congress Party. He united the Hindus and Muslims and started the Non-co-operation movement. They shunned foreign clothes, government services, councils, courts, schools, colleges and degrees. However, there were some members in the Congress who had no faith in the policy of non-co-operation and they were in favour of participating in the councils and the houses of Lords. Later Chittranjan Das and Motilal Nehru established a separate institution and named it as the Swaraj Party. On the other hand Congress intended to appease the Muslim community. Therefore Madan Mohan Malviya, Lajpat Rai and other leaders joined the Hindu Mahasabha. During this period Mohammed Ali Jinnah left the Congress and joined the Muslim League. The merciless acts of the Britishers continued in the same cruel manner up to the Twenties and Thirties. A terrible religious conflict took place in 1930 in which a student Ganesh Shanker had to sacrifice his life. The period that followed (1931-35) was one of commissions, discussions and agreements. The elections were held in 1937 and in the majority of Indian States, the Congress formed the ministry. However, in 1939 they had to submit their resignation as the British Government (without the permission of the Indians) announced the involvement of India in the Second World War. In 1940 the demand of Pakistan was made. In order to get the Indian assistance the Cripps Proposals (1942) were made, which were outrightly rejected. In 1942 Congress passed the Quit India Resolution, which led to imprisonment of innumerable leaders. The year 1945 had a democratic British Government that sympathized with the Indian Independence Movement. As a result, an Interim government was formed in India (1946). Around this time, on account of the scornful policy of the Muslim League, Calcutta, Noakhali, Bihar and Punjab witnessed terrible riots. On the Fifteenth August 1947, India achieved Independence. But this light was stained with the vivisection of the subcontinent.

1.1.3. *Economic Conditions of the Indian Renaissance*

After 1857 the English Rule was firmly established in India, as a result of which the economic organization and culture of the eighteenth century gradually began to disappear. In the second half of the eighteenth century, there were a number of industrial establishments, which the Britishers destroyed, thereby hindering our social and economic progress.[19] The aim of the Britishers was economic exploitation of India by destroying our indigenous business establishments and on the other hand they began setting up new industries with their currency. The introduction of railways, the posts and telegraphs was basically made to suit their economic and political progress. The spread of education too was motivated essentially for the production of cheap clerks. Soaring prices, famine, taxes and poverty were the major economic problems that confronted the Indian Renaissance, and its echo in modern literature is but natural. That was the reason that prompted the Congress to demand economic independence along with political independence. After the Sepoy's Mutiny (1857), the Britishers adopted a policy of favouring the landlords and denying justice to the peasants and the farmers' community. Some patriots like Premanand, Premnarayan, Ambikadatt Vyas and many others believed that the import of foreign goods was responsible for the poor economic conditions of India. Premanand's *Aryabhinanadan*, Premnarayan Mishra's *Holi Hae*, and Ambikadatt Vyas's *Bharat Dharma* indicate that the root cause of our poor economic condition is the purchase of the foreign items. Bharatendu also depicts the familial, social and national deterioration of the economy of India in his works.[20]

Most of the patriots and reformers criticized the moral duplicity of British Government and exploitation of economic resources of India. The Britishers used the Indian resources as the raw material for their industries and sold their ready-made items at higher prices to the Indians to exploit them economically. The era following the First World War brought a marked change in the Congress and its policies. They shunned the use of foreign clothes and opposed the British Industrial Policy and economic exploitation. This is obviously reflected in the works of contemporary Indian English writers like Tagore, Aurobindo, Gandhi, Nehru and many others. The end of the Second World War brought widespread unemployment and soaring prices of essential and primary commodities. The capitalists' propaganda resulted in the exploitation of the peasant and labour class. The Britishers, then, brought changes in their economic policy in order to fulfil their expansionist aims. They also developed Indian industries though the exploitation continued on the same scale.

1.1.4. *Literary Conditions of the Indian Renaissance*

The discovery of the printing press brought about a tremendous change in world literature. The literature of the Indian Renaissance was the literature of cultural reawakening. Its poetry as well as prose expressed the spirit of the age. The Indian Renaissance provided new vision and new direction to the literature of the age. The literature of the age manifested human emotions such as patriotism, love, national consciousness, unity and brotherhood. During the medieval period the literature was primarily religious in nature and content. It was written for 'Shivetarkshataye' and for 'Parmanand.'[21] But as the writers of the Indian Renaissance came into contact with western culture and literature, their literature began specifically having a social backdrop. It centralized human life and focused on the social evils, political dependence, its consequent-agony and yearning for independence and humanism.

The Indian Renaissance literature in direct relevance to the eighteenth century literature differs in content and style of the preceding ages. The reason for this difference, on the one hand, though is political, social, economical and religious awareness, on the other, there equally stands the profound impact of world literature with its diversities. The majority of the works of the medieval period had an aristocratic upbringing as compared to Modern Indian literature that speaks of the common men's feelings of happiness and sorrow. The middle period was dominated by restrictions, inhibitions and was limited in content while the nineteenth century Indian literature depicted a wider range of thought, content and imagery. As a result of which it saw the entire humanity with its naked eyes.

In Gujarat Narmad, Dalpatram, Karsandas Moolji, Govardhanram Tripathi, Mansukhram Tripathi, Manilal Dwivedi, Navalram Pandya initiated measures for bringing about social awareness and reformation. Narmad, who has been regarded as the Father of Gujarati prose started taking concrete steps for creating the reformative atmosphere through his newsletter *Dandiyo* in 1864.[22] Narmad's poem *Hinduoni Padati* is considered to be the Bible of reformation. His poem 'Jay Garvi Gujarat' is well known for his love of his motherland. He became the forerunner of social awakening and reformative activities.

Dalpatram aroused the Indians through his works and his magazine *Buddhiprakash*. He wrote essays on *Bhoot Nibandh*, *Gyati Nibandh* and *Bal Vivah* expressing the protest against the prevailing superstitions and ideas.[23] Karsandas Moolji wrote his articles in his magazine *Satya Prakash* and tried to reform the society. Govardhanram Tripathi, Mansukhram Tripathi, Manilal Dwivedi and Navalram Pandya also attempted to promote reformative activities. Navalram Pandya was the first teacher who considered the name and work of a teacher as of a high rank. He started his critical writing as the editor of 'Gujarat Shala Patra'[24] Forbse and Dalpatram and afterwards Acharya Yashvant Shukla continued the tradition of the 'Gujarat Vernacular Society' which was founded by Forbse in 1848. They started a weekly 'Vartaman Patra.'

Narmad and his friends established the 'Buddhivardhak Sabha' in 1851. It hastened the activites of social reformation and women's education. Narmad continued the lecture system in order to carry out the work of reformation. Dadabhai Navroji and other young men under the guidance of Petan Saheb founded the 'Gyan Prakash sabha.' Its main goal was to encourage women's education and social work. Several other newspapers and magazines such as *Stri-Bodh, Prajabandhu* and *Gujarati Panch* were also published. In 1880, *Gujarati* weekly, in 1881, *Kesare Hind,* in 1888 *Kathiawad Times,* in 1895 *Sayaji Vijay* and in 1902 *Sanj Vartaman* were started as the part of the Swaraj movement. Gandhiji wrote articles on Truth, non-violence, inter-caste marriage, upliftment of Harijans, Hindu-Muslim equality and Savinay-Kanoon Bhang.

In Hindi the first newsletter *Udant Martand* was started in 1826 by Jugal Kishore Sukul. In 1846 M. Nasiruddin edited *Jagat Deepak Bhaskar.* In 1844 *Baneras Akhbar* was started which Taramohan Mitra edited. There were many other newsletters, newspapers and magazines that strove to promote the Indian Renaissance movement. For instance in Bengal, the editorship of *The Hindoo Patriot* came to Kristo Das. Bipin Chandra Pal (1834-84) then headed the paper with great distinction for almost a quarter century, under whose energetic leadership the Brahmo-Samaj movement spread. Keshub Chander Sen (1838-84) started the fortnightly *Indian Mirror,* in 1861. He emphasized the essential unity of all religions. Bankim wrote his *Anand Math* under the influence of a forty-six page autobiography by Vasudeo Balvantray Phadke, who had revolted against the Britishers in the days of the Deccan famine of 1876-77. Bankim Chandra Chatterjee (1838-94), a renowned Bengali novelist, wrote several essays in English, including *On the Origin of Hindu Festivals, Bengali Literature, The Study of Hindu Philosophy* and *Vedic Literature.* Vyomesh Chander Banerjee (1844-1906) the first President of the Indian National Congress (1855), established the London Indian Society in 1865. Motilal Ghose (1847-1902) founded the well-known newspaper, *Amrit Bazaar Patrika* in 1868. Romesh Chander Dutt (1848-1909) was a pioneer in both the literatures of travel and literary history. Surendranath Banerjee (1848-1925) was a powerful orator in English, who convened the first National Conference in 1883, which became the harbinger of the Indian National Congress. He was an outstanding moderate leader who eclipsed only with the rise of Gandhi. His *Speeches* and autobiography embodied in *A Nation in Making* are remarkable. Tracing the reminiscences of fifty years of public life (1925), he claimed to have had a high patriotic purpose; *viz.*, to trace the growth of the National Movement and to do justice to the early builders of the nation. Bipin Chandra Pal, one of the celebrated radical trio called 'Lal-Bal-Pal' (Lala Lajpat Rai, Bal Gangadhar Tilak, Bipin Chandra Pal) wrote both on politics in *Nationality and Empire*, (1916); *Indian Nationalism: Its Principles and Personalities* (1919) and on religion in his *Introduction to the Study of Hinduism* (1908). Chittaranjan Das (1870-1925), who came to be known as 'Deshbandhu' also wrote both lyrical verse and prose in Bengali.

Another trio comprises of Rabindranath Tagore, Vivekananda and Aurobindo Ghose. The earliest prose writing of Tagore was *Sadhana* (1913). His other two collections of speeches are *Personality* (1917) and *Nationalism* (1917). In these lectures, we have a clear formation of Tagore's philosophical position regarding nation and nationalism of the western kind. He discusses the age-old problem of evil, and indicates the way to the realization of the Infinite, through intermediate stages such as realization in love, in action and in beauty.

Vivekananda in his lectures inspires his countrymen to arise, awake and not stop till the goal is attained. He, in his visionary writeup *Rebuild India* asks the New Indians to arise out of peasants' cottage, to grasp the plough out of the huts of the fishermen, the cobbler and the sweeper. The New Indians should spring from the grocer's shop, from beside the oven of the fritter-celler, from the factory, from marts, from markets, from forests, from hills and mountains. Vivekananda asks his countrymen to keep their eyes and ears open. And no sooner they do this, they would hear the inaugural shout of Renaissant India, ringing with the voice of a million thunders and reverberating throughout the universe.

Aurobindo had come under the influence of Vivekananda and produced an enormous and varied mass of prose writings on religious, metaphysical, occult, social, political, cultural and literary subjects. Shelley's poem, *The Revolt of Islam* helped to turn Aurobindo's maturing thought in the direction of political action. Touched by something in Shelley's imaginative recreation of the French revolution, Aurobindo decided to dedicate his life 'to a similar world-change and take part in it.'[25] Aurobindo's father had also begun to send him newspaper reports of the mistreatment of Indians by Britons. When Aurobindo learnt about the conditions in his homeland, his general commitment to revolutionary action was:

> 'canalised into the idea of the liberation of his own country.'[26]

While in *The Renaissance in India*, he asks his countrymen to,

> [...] admit Western science, reason, progressiveness, the essential modern ideas, but on the basis of our own way of life and assimilated to our spiritual aim and ideal [...].[27]

In 1903, he wrote a booklet entitled *No Compromise* and began working as the editor of the *Bande Matram* in 1906. The newspaper soon became the herald of the Indian revolution. Mr. Ratcliffe, the then editor of *The Statesman,* says that *Bande Matram* was:

> [...] the most effective voice of what we then called nationalist extremism.[28]

In 1907, the Government prosecuted the *Bande Matram* and Aurobindo as its editor for propagating sedition. It was a country-wide sensation. Tagore then wrote his poem on Aurobindo:

> Rabindranath, O Aurobindo, bows to thee! [...].

And a few years later when Tagore met Aurobindo at the latter's ashram, he wrote:

> Aurobindo, accept the salutation of Rabindra.[29]

He also published an *Open Letter to My Countrymen,* in which he opposed the Minto-Morley reforms. He founded the monthly *Arya.* His other prominent writings include *New Lamps for Old,* and *The Renaissance in India* and others. The hopeful picture of India is explicit in Aurobindo's words:

> The process which has led up to the renaissance now inevitable, may be analysed, both historically and logically, into three steps by which a transition is being managed, a complex breaking reshaping and new building, with the final result yet distant in prospect,—though here and there the first bases may have been already laid,—a new age of an old culture transformed, not an affiliation of a new-born civilization to one that is old and dead, but a true rebirth, a renascence [...].[30]

1.2. A Brief Survey of Indo-English Poetry (1857—1950)

It is a well-known fact that the introduction of English education in India caused a tremendous ferment in the life and literature of the people. The landing of Vasco-da-gama in Kerela in 1498, the arrival of father Stephens in Goa in 1579[31] and the landing of the British East India Company in Bombay in 1668[32] caused the exchange of several Indian words into Portuguese and also into English. By the end of the seventeenth century, a number of Indian words had been acclimatized into English. And by the end of the eighteenth century, Englishmen in India had started writing poetry on local Indian subjects.

Indian Poetry in English commenced in Bengal, the province in which the British first secured a stronghold. For the first fifty years it was limited entirely to a few Bengali families who were inhabitants of the city and progressively it moved to other cities such as Madras and Bombay. On the other hand Anglo-Indian literature (Literature written by the English in India) came to an end with India's independence. Gradually, on account of the literature written by the Indians in English the Indian critics argued for a special identity for Indian literature in English. They who were influenced by the freedom struggle made this demand in the 1930s and 1940s. The most influential among these was K.R.S. Iyengar whose *Indo-Anglian Literature* was the first elaborate discussion of this literature as a distinct, independent field of study. He used the term 'Indo-Anglian' to suggest that it was a part of Indian Literature rather than British Literature.[33] In essence, Indo-English literature has had an illustrious history and it includes many literary forms from the epic to the personal essay. It is regarded as a part of Indian Literature. Makarand Paranjape rightly states:

> It is reasonable, then, to regard Indian Poetry in English as the limb of the larger body of Indian Poetry, a creation of a sensibility similar to that which produced the regional language poetry in India. Perhaps the best proof of the close affinity between Indian poetry in English and the poetry in regional languages is the fact that most of the Indian poets in English have been bilingual or have at least translated from Indian languages. The list of these includes Toru Dutt, Manmohan Ghose, Sri Aurobindo, Rabindranath Tagore, Puran Singh, Sri Anand Acharya, Nisim Ezekiel, A.K. Ramanujan, R. Parthasarathy, Pritish Nandy, A.K. Mehrotra, Arun Kolatkar, Jayanta Mahapatra, Dilip Chitre, Salim Peeradina, and Agha Sahid Ali. These poets have enriched both the source languages from which they translate and the target language, English. Yet, we must never forget that because it is written in a language not fully Indian, Indian poetry in English will always remain a frontier or boundary literature, the middle ground between the West and India, the site of conflicting tensions and pulls.[34]

The first among Indo-English poets was Henry Louis Vivian Derozio. He was Indian not only by birth but also by self-definition. His love for India is revealed in several of his poems. His sonnets, *The Harp of India* and *To India—My Native Land*, are regarded as fine examples of India's earliest nationalistic poetry. He was strongly influenced by the English romantics and he influenced Bengali poets. He has won for himself a niche in the history of Indo-English poetry.

Another pioneering Indo-English poet was Kashiprasad Ghose who published, *Shiar and Other Poems*. He was the first Hindu to write original English verse.

Michael Madhusudan Dutt was a passionate admirer of Byron and sent poems to Blackwood's Magazine dedicating them to Wordsworth. Two longer pieces, *The Captive Ladie* and *Vision of Past* and some sonnets and lyrics form his contribution to Indian Writing in English.

Romesh Chander Dutt translated the *Ramayana* and *Mahabharata* into felicitous English verse. He also published his *Lays of Ancient India* in 1894.

There were also some minor poets who show a wonderful command over the English language and the metrical systems but they lacked the vigour and imagination of a true poet. They were Navakissen Ghose, Nizanath Zung, Roby Dutt, Manikram Vasanmal Thadani, P. Sheshadri and Govind Krishna Chettur.

Aru Dutt and Toru Dutt were gifted sisters. They were the inheritors of unfulfilled renown. They were poets of rare promise with no insignificant achievement. Toru was a genius in Indian English Poetry. She contributed a volume entitled, *A Sheaf Gleaned in French Fields.* She also wrote short lyrics, odes and sonnets. Aru wrote a few pieces including *Morning Serenade,* which filled Edmund Gosse with surprise and rapture. Toru Dutt's *Ancient Ballads and Legends of Hindustan* appeared posthumously in 1882, which proved her proficiency and power of poetic utterance in a foreign medium. The story of *Sita* and other mythical characters is told with a new freshness and charm. This was for the first time that an Indian girl enshrined the old stories in English verse.

Manmohan Ghose was unique among Indian writers of English verse. His poetry is entirely western in taste and allusion. He wrote two poetic sequences—*Immortal Eve* and *Orphic Mysteries,* which almost irradiate the true pathos and sublimity of true poetry. His poems appeared in *Primavera* during his stay at Oxford.

Rabindranath Tagore is regarded as the titan among the Indian writers of English verse. Basically he was a Bengali poet, but he had translated his verse into English prose. He had written a few original English verses as well where one finds beauty of rhythm and movement. Even his prose translations are full of rhythmic beauty and wealth of imagery. His lyrics are marked by spontaneous flow, delicacy, exuberance of fancy, radiant clarity and grace of diction, charm and poignancy of feeling and abundance of natural imagery. His numerous volumes, such as *Gitanjali* (1912), *The Crescent Moon* (1913), *Fruit Gathering* (1916), *The Gardener* (1913) and others, prove his talent as a very good poet. His poems are strikingly finished, rich in texture and profound in thought.

Aurobindo Ghose, the younger brother of Manmohan Ghose, was more than a poet. He was a patriot, philosopher, and yogi rolled into one. He wrote in almost every available genre—lyrics, sonnets, long narrative poems, dramatic poetry and epic. The two impressive volumes of his *Collected Poems and Plays* (1942) contained work that had been written as early as the eighteen nineties and were also recent experiments in quantitative verse. As a translator and narrative poet, as a daring experimenter and explorer, and above all, as a futurist poet, Aurobindo had a record of poetic achievement without a parallel in his time. *Urvasie* and *Love and Death* are nobly eloquent narrative poems while *Baji Prabhou* is a first rate poem of action. *The Rose of God* and *Thoughts the Paradate* are among the finest mystical poems in the language. His supreme achievement was *Savitri,* a colossal epic running to about 24,000 lines.

The history of Indian poetry in English remains unfulfilled without the name of Sarojini Naidu. Her poetical output is contained in the volumes called, *The Golden Threshold* (1905), *The Bird of Time* (1912), *The Broken Wing* (1917). These volumes are full of heartfelt feeling and picturesque Indian imagery. Her genius was essentially lyrical and her poetry full of music. She was remarkably versatile. She was chiefly a love poet and her poetry explores the many facets of love as outlined in classical texts: love in union, love in longing, love in separation, the pain of love, the sin of love, desire of love, earthly love and divine love. There one finds at times the introduction of a note of mysticism, of philosophy and of the supernatural.

Harindranath Chattopadhyay was one of the youngest writers of English verse. His *The Feast of Youth* (1918), *Coloured Garden* (1919), *The Magic Tree, Perfume of Earth, Ancient Wings* and *Grey Clouds* and *White Showers* (1922-24), all these volumes contain lyrics of a reflective and philosophic nature. His output is varied in theme ranging from Aurobindonian idealism to Marxist materialism, but his formal range is narrow.

The post-Independence poetry in English has acquired a

distinct character and voice of its own. Good poetry was produced during this period. The base was expanded and higher standards were enforced. The dominant tone and taste shifted. The noted Indo-English poets of this period are—Dom Moraes, Nissim Ezekiel, P. Lal, Kamala Das, Shiv K. Kumar, Keki N. Daruwalla, A.K. Ramanujan, R. Parthasarathy, Pritish Nandy, Gauri Deshpande and Jayanta Mahapatra. These poets rejected the past and opposed the idealism and romanticism of their predecessors. They introduced a bold new frankness into their poetry. They turned from religion to their personal relationships. The work of these recent Indo-English poets displays the colours of modernity, thematic variety and superb craftsmanship. Recent Indo-English Poetry is genuine because it is deeply felt and addressed to the whole community. Indian situations form a vital part of it. The poets write exclusively of their private lives, the detachment of the alienated speaker, identity-crisis, tradition-modernity conflict and of the present day world. The most popular of examples of this category are, Ezekiel's *Background* and *Hymns in Darkness,* Shiv Kumar's *Broken Columns, Subterfuges* and *To a Prostitute,* Parthasarathy's *Rough Passage* and Homecoming, Ramanujan's *Self Portrait* and *Selected Poems,* and Kamala Das's *An Introduction* and *The Sunshine Cat,* Jussawala's *Approaching Shanta Cruz Airport, Bombay,* Gieve Patel's *Hill Station,* Daruwalla's *Routine* and *Crossing of Rivers,* Mahapatra's *Dawn at Puri,* Chitre's *Father Returning Home,* and Kolatkar's *Jejuri.* The quest for cultural moorings also seems to be a major preoccupation of these poets. They speak of love and sex, as an inseparable part of life. Kamala Das's *The Looking Glass,* Shiv Kumar's *The Sun Temple of Konark,* Ezekiel's *Nudes* etc. are fine examples of this type. Shiv Kumar's *Poet Laureate* and *Cabaret Dancer,* Ezekiel's *Guru* and many other poems are replete with ironic humour.

1.3. Literary Output of Tagore and Aurobindo

Rabindranath Tagore, the heralder of the new mode of schooling and learning was born at Jorasanko, Calcutta on 7th May, 1861. As the son of Maharishi Devendranath and Sarala Devi, he inherited a rich and vast tradition where mythology, theology and philosophy blended easily. His education began rather early and he was sent to the Calcutta Training Academy and then to the Normal School.[35] Observing that Rabindranath was not very keen in adapting himself to the educational environment of the times his parents sent him to the University of London where he studied for a year and a half. But on account of the solid grounding that he received in Bengali, Sanskrit and English he began composing and writing on his own. His deep interest in music and wrestling kept him mentally and physically fit. His father's love of nature and sense of beauty also profoundly inspired him.

Rabindranath's boyhood was a mixture of unusual happenings and experiences. Inspite of being made to live in the company of servants, he had received by way of inheritance a brand of thinking, which was radical and rational in nature. The path shown by his Vedic ancestors had made him more temperamental than traditional. His deep study of the Indian religious texts; European and English literature, had made him absorb the best of the East and the West. His short sojourn in England laid the foundation to the early creations of Tagore. On his return to India he found himself caught in the winds of the Indian Renaissance.

The *Evening Songs* (1881), and the *Morning Songs* (1884), mark the real beginning of his poetic career. *Offerings* (1901) and *The Ferry* (1901) are the best collections of this period. The year 1901 was very important in Tagore's life. He founded the Shantiniketan on the model of the gurukulas, at Bholpur. This open-air school turned into a University—the Vishwa-Bharati, in 1920. However, successive bereavements—the death of his wife, daughter, disciple, father and son, in between 1902 and 1907 induced in him a mood of solitary confinement and renunciation. For a while he toyed with politics, but finding that many did not share his views and ideology he remained in silent meditation for a year, only to emerge with his masterpiece—the *Gitanjali.* The work brought him in contact with G.B. Shaw, H.G. Wells, Galsworthy, Masefield, Robert Bridges, W.B. Yeats and a number of other celebrities. The English translation of the work won him the Nobel Prize for literature in 1913. This period marks the full flowering of his genius. His chief works include, *The Crescent Moon* (1913), *The Gardener* (1913), *Songs of Kabir* (1915), *Fruit Gathering*

(1916), *Lover's Gift* (1918), *Crossing* (1918) and *The Fugitive and Other Poems* (1921), *The Genius of Valmiki* (1881), *The Fateful Hunt* (1882), *The Play of Illusions* (1888), *The King and the Queen* (1889), *Sacrifice* (1890), *Chitrangada* (1892), *The Appeal of Gandhari* (1897), *The King of the Dark Chamber* (1910), *Cycle of Spring* (1916), *Free Current* (1922), *Red Oleanders* (1925), and *House Warming* (1925). Tagore also has a number of philosophical works as *Sadhana* (1913), *Nationalism* (1917), *Personality* (1917), *Creative Unity* (1922), *The Religion of Man* (1931), and *Man* (1932), and a few novels as *The Young Queen's Mart* (1883). The *Royal Sage* (1887), *Eye Sore* (1903), *The Wreck* (1906), *Gora* (1909), *The Home and the World* (1916) to his credit.

The strain of mysticism, humanism and religion is seen in almost all the works mentioned above. However, the Hibbert Lectures at Oxford can be taken as definite and authoritative in the sense that these lectures specifically dwell on his religion—the religion of man, while in his poetry the religion is to be inferred. Tagore believed that his religious life had followed the same mysterious line of growth, as had his poetical life. His religion was neither ready-made nor tailor made. A confluence of natural and manly attributes in relation to his personal deity and civilization; ever receptive to fresh winds and unorthodox in nature and approach, designed the text of his religion. He was a man who had drunk the waters of many rivers and yet he was never satisfied. His religion transcended the barriers of caste and creed; race and colour. Although traces and influences right from the *Bhagavad Gita*, the Vedas and the Upanishads, the songs of Kabir, to the Vaishnava saints, the sufi mystics and Buddhism, can be found in the religion of Tagore, it essentially is a very human religion. A religion which strove to assert that liberation can be attained 'here and now.' His cri de coeur, the poet's faith and belief was to that extent original, authentic and out of the ordinary.

The vision that Tagore had when he was just emerging out of his teens (*The Awakening of the Waterfall*) had made the theistic theme quite apparent but definitely not dominant in all his early poetical creations. In retrospect Tagore often felt that some Being had comprehended him and his world in all his experiences. The central idea that governed his religion of man was the humanness of the Supreme Being. He felt that such an entity should necessarily be an embodiment of compassion and lovc. One who should be able to see the suffering humanity and at the same time be able to identify himself with them. This centre of Unity and relationship formed the introductory text of his familial religion.

The religion of man was not to be a forum for sorting out ideological differences or putting an end to petty rivalries. It had nothing to do with any tenet of the existing religious systems that denigrated the importance of human beings. He was much closer to Wordsworth, Whitman and Blake in the sense that he again and again referred to the human faculty of imagination, which critics often associate with intuition or the vision divine. The sole objective of the human being lay in his ceaseless progress and development at the mental and spiritual levels. To him realization was of utmost importance.

The theory of evolution, designed to meet the rational human needs, was also equally acceptable to Tagore, though the dimension he added was purely psychological in nature. It was more of a voyage within than without. A journey that required a proper understanding of the underlying unity of God, Man and Nature. This all-pervasive consciousness was the edifice on which Tagore built his religion. He felt that a person's cognitive faculty when coupled with imagination could lead him to realize the unattained in this very life. Man through dedicated soul-searching was capable of viewing his deeper-self (the truth of his being; the heaven of his freedom) and realizing the futility of the physical and the impertinence of the flesh. Love between man and woman is one of Nature's laws, and it can neither be avoided nor can its pace be forced. *Chitra* in particular is the quint-essence of romance. The drama presents the evolution of human love from the physical/sensual to the spiritual. Salvation or Nirvana was, thus, to be attained to elevate the society as a whole and it was not meant to be for mere personal progress. For Tagore, in contrast to Spinoza, the Ideal was always the more real. His concern was centred more on an ideal civilization than on the actual society. It was with this yardstick that he equated himself with his contemporaries and later when he found that not everyone had reached the shores of superhumanhood, he was disillusioned. Life for Tagore was an unceasing pilgrimage that concluded with death—the revealer of eternity; the fulfilment of life. All so-called barriers between God, Man and Nature were artificial and nothing could separate their Unity. He doubted if there was anything real in and about individual separateness from God. Nothing short of human perfection governed his criteria of Truth and Spirituality. To him true humanism involved genuine spirituality.

Tagore was one of the most versatile man of his age. He was the first Indian poet and writer who gained a permanent place for modern India on the world literary map. He played various roles during his long and fruitful career as a poet, dramatist, novelist, short story writer, composer, painter, thinker, educationist, nationalist and internationalist. Jawaharlal Nehru opined that Tagore was in line with the rishis, the great sages of India, drawing from the wisdom of the ancient past and giving it a practical garb and meaning in the present. The most prominent theme in almost all his poetical works revolves around the relation between the finite and the infinite. To him, God is no remote Absolute but an entity emboding *Sat, Chit* and *Aananda* and the universe a joyous expression of God's play and human love a step to the divine.

On the other hand, Aurobindo, the experimentalist and the modernist, was born on 15th August 1872 in Calcutta. He was the son of Dr. Krishna Dhan Ghose and Swarnalata Devi. His maternal grandfather was Rajnarain Bose who after coming into contact with Devendranath Tagore, the father of Rabindranath Tagore, became a member of the Brahmo Samaj. In 1877, Aurobindo together with his two elder brothers was sent to Loretto Convent School at Darjeeling. In 1879, they went to Manchester where Reverend William H. Drewett and Mrs. Drewett taught Aurobindo. In 1884, Aurobindo was admitted to St. Paul's School. In 1890, he went to King's College, Cambridge where he composed a number of poems, which were published in the *Fox Family Magazine* of Manchester.[36] In 1892, he left Cambridge for London. He was expected to join the I.C.S. but repeated failures in the riding test disqualified him. He left England in 1893 and joined service of the Maharaja of Baroda. This period was literally very productive.

Aurobindo, had a career that extended to six decades till his death in 1950. His activities related to yoga greatly spurred his creativity and led to the birth *of Songs to Myrtilla and Other Poems* (1895), *Poems* (1905), *Ahanu and Other Poems* (1915), *Poems: Past and Present* (1946), *Songs of Vidyapati* (1956), *Ilion* (1957), *Rodogune* (1958), *The Vaziers of Bassora* (1958), *Savitri: A Legend and A Symbol* (1950), *The Renaissance in India* (1920), *The Life Divine* (1950), *The Synthesis of Yoga* (1948), *Essays on the Gita* (1922), *On the Veda* (1956), *The Ideal of Human Unity* (1919), *The Human Cycle* (1949), *The Future Poetry* (1953), and *The Foundations of Indian Culture* (1953), which have an unmatched form of variety of thought and content in the entire range of Indian English Literature. Of the vast poetical output *Savitri* represents a product of a lifetime; a cosmic artistic work with supramental realms and cosmic dimensions, which illumines every important concern of mankind. His early works *viz., Urvasie* and *Love and Death* had set the tenour for this masterpiece.

Aurobindo is primarily known for his monumental epic *Savitri.* His in-depth study of the English language gave him an unsurpassed authority and command over its use, apart from his mastery of the Greek, Latin and Sanskrit Literatures. He is known for his bulk of excellent verse; his use of quantative metre (*Savitri*) and his capacity of laying bare a rhythmic life beyond the ranges of inspired consciousness. He stands out as the creator of a new Vedic and Upanishadic age of poetry. His views found consonance with the Vedic poets, the Hindu legends and myths, that always spoke of the inherent divine nature of man. He also felt the necessity of turning the spark into the flame during one's lifetime. To Aurobindo, poetry belonged to a higher order, the practice of which would turn a poet into a seer and a prophet. This evolution of consciousness would in turn lead him to create poetry of a mystical kind. To him the objective of poetry was not to instruct or pursue knowledge but to have a life of its own; to embody beauty and to give delight and it was to be directed towards personal growth and self-development of man.

Aurobindo had swiftly outgrown the romantic and decadent influence of Keats, Shelley and Swinburne, and this departure from influenced writings is first observed in *Perseus, the*

Deliverer, whose after-effects looms large in *Savitri.* The theme of deliverance continued in some of the pre-Savitri works. Love forms the key motif in *Urvasie, Love and Death* and *Chitrangada.* These sublime sagas are based on episodes from Indian mythology. However, with *Savitri* there is a marked change in Aurobindo's attitude towards love, which has become neo-symbolic and natural; comprehensive and encompassing; spiritual and mystical. The poems in *Songs to Myrtilla* carry some of the most beautiful descriptions of nature. The vivid portrayal of natural phenomena with minute details illustrates his power of observation.

Aurobindo was one of the great seers of the country, who firmly held the bow of creative energy. Even if we consider Aurobindo as a poet and a critic of poetry, he would still rank among the Supreme masters of our time. *Savitri* makes man's life intelligible in the cosmos, shows Love as Power wedded to Grace, demonstrates the possibilities of the death of Death, and projects man's future in a changed and transformed earth.

Both Tagore and Aurobindo, were the modern spokesmen of humanism, universalism and of the oneness of man. They were complete human beings and their intellectual flowering and spiritual fullness is emphatically observed in *Chitra* and *Savitri* respectively. Their poetical thought is thus strongly rooted in the tenets of Indian religion and philosophy, which needs, to be understood, felt and experienced at the physical, mental and spiritual levels.

1.4. Objectives of the Study

The present dissertation endeavours to study *Chitra* and *Savitri* comparatively taking into consideration the content, the form, and the philosophy of the two works. It proposes to study the gradual evolution taking place in the personalities of *Chitra* and *Savitri,* the heroines of the play and the epic respectively, which in turn is essentially a mirror of the mental and spiritual growth of both Tagore and Aurobindo. The aim of this thesis is to work out the causes of similarity and dissimilarity in the personalities of the two heroines. That only self-knowledge, which begins at the physical level and moves upward to the mental and spiritual levels, is the final basis of liberation, forms the basis of discussion in the chapters to follow.

The first chapter introduces the poets Tagore and Aurobindo; traces the social, cultural, religious, economic, political and literary conditions of the Indian Renaissance; provides a brief survey of Indo-English poetry and finally examines the literary output of Tagore and Aurobindo in order to evaluate their comparative position.

The second chapter outlines the content of *Chitra* and *Savitri*. Herein the theme, the character, the symbolic interpretation along with the variations between the original legend and the composition by the writers are worked out.

The third chapter is a study in form. It traces the characteristics of the drama and the epic form written in the West and the East and places *Chitra* and *Savitri* in perspective.

The fourth chapter brings out the consciousness of *Chitra* and *Savitri*, through philosophical analysis and studies how Chitra and Savitri overcome their Illusion and Ignorance respectively.

And the last chapter discusses the characters of Chitra and Savitri from an Indian feministic point of view and arrives at the conclusion that *Chitra* and *Savitri* are essentially the two sides of the same coin—*nari-chetana.*

REFERENCES

1. V.D. Mahajan, *History of Medieval India* (New Delhi: S. Chand and Co.: 1988), 336.
2. V.D. Mahajan, *History of Medieval India* (New Delhi: S. Chand and Co.: 1988), 353.
3. Bacchan Singh, *Aadhunik Hindi Sahitya Ka Itihas* (Allahabad: Lokbharti Prakashan: 1977), 15.
4. Bacchan Singh. *Aadhunik Hindi Sahitya Ka Itihas* (Allahabad: Lokbharti Prakashan: 1977), 7.
5. Dr. Ganapatichandra Gupta, "Purvapithika," *Hindi Sahitya Ka Itihas*, ed. Dr. Nagendra (Allahabad: National Publishing House: 1976), 61.
6. Bachhan Singh, *Adhunik Hindi Sahitya Ka Itihas* (Allahabad: Lokbharti Prakashan: 1977), 10.
7. Dr. Ramesh M. Trivedi, *Arvachin Gujarati Sahitya No Itihas* (Ahmedabad: Adarsh Prakashan: 1993-94), 10.
8. Bachhan Singh, *Adhunik Hindi Sahitya Ka Itihas* (Allahabad: Lokbharti Prakashan: 1977): 28.

9. *Ibid.*, 29.
10. *Ibid.*, 29.
11. Dr. Ramesh M. Trivedi, *Arvachin Gujarati Sahitya No Itihas* (Ahmedabad: Adarsh Prakashan: 1993-94), 5.
12. Bachhan Singh, *Adhunik Hindi Sahitya Ka Itihas* (Allahabad: Lokbharti Prakashan: 1977), 31.
13. *Ibid.*, 31.
14. *Ibid.*, 30.
15. Manoj Das, *Sri Aurobindo* (New Delhi: Sahitya Akademi: 1972), 26.
16. *Ibid.*, 37.
17. Dr. Ramesh M. Trivedi, *Arvachin Gujarati Sahitya No Itihas* (Ahmedabad: Adarsh Prakashan: 1993-94), 6.
18. Peter Heehs, *Sri Aurobindo: A Brief Biography* (Delhi: Oxford University Press: 1993): 5.
19. Bachhan Singh, *Adhunik Hindi Sahitya Ka Itihas* (Allahabad: Lokbharti Prakashan: 1977): 17.
20. Dr. Sureshchandra Gupta, "Bhartendu-Yug," *Hindi Sahitya Ka Itihas*, ed. Dr. Nagendra (Allahabad: National Publishing House: 1976), 462.
21. Dr. Ramesh M. Trivedi, *Arvachin Gujarati Sahitya No Itihas* (Ahmedabad: Adarsh Prakashan: 1993-94), 3.
22. *Ibid.*, 7.
23. *Ibid.*, 18-21.
24. *Ibid.*, 40.
25. Peter Heehs, *Sri Aurobindo* (Delhi: Oxford University Press: 1993), 11.
26. *Ibid.*, 11.
27. Sri Aurobindo, *Sri Aurobindo on India* (Pondicherry: Sri Aurobindo's Action: 1973) 79.
28. Manoj Das, *Sri Aurobindo* (New Delhi: Sahitya Akademi: 1972) 35.
29. *Ibid.*, 38, 45.
30. Sri Aurobindo, *Sri Aurobindo on India* (Pondicherry: Sri Aurobindo's Action: 1973), 70-71.
31. Makarand Paranjape, *Indian Poetry in English* (Bangalore: Macmillan India Limited: 1993), 1.
32. V.D. Mahajan, *History of Medieval India* (New Delhi: S. Chand and Co.: 1988), 176.
33. Makarand Paranjape, *Indian Poetry in English* (Bangalore: Macmillan India Limited: 1993), 4.
34. *Ibid.*, 5.
35. Dipankar Chattopadhyay, *Introduction to Tagore* (Calcutta: Vishwabharati: 1988) 63.
36. Manoj Das, *Sri Aurobindo* (New Delhi: Sahitya Akademi: 1972), 9.

2

Tagore's *Chitra* and Aurobindo's *Savitri*: A Study in Content

This chapter endeavours to systematically examine the points of comparison in terms of legend, theme, character and symbolic interpretation between *Chitra* and *Savitri*. A beginning is made with tracing the original legend in the *Mahabharata* and then outlining the change in the treatment of the stories by Tagore and Aurobindo respectively. Further, the variations between the original legends and the text are worked out systematically. And finally the corresponding and the differentiating points between *Chitra* and *Savitri* are presented.

2. THE CHITRA LEGEND

Manipureshwaram Rajan dharmagyam Chitravahanam
Tasya Chitrangada nama duhita charudarshana[1]

Chitra is based on the *Mahabharata* legend of Chitrangada and Arjuna. Arjuna came to Manipur during the course of his wanderings to fulfil a vow of penance. He saw Chitrangada, the beautiful daughter of Chitravahana, the king of the country and was captivated by her charming beauty. He then asked the king for the hand of his daughter in marriage. The king asked him to reveal his identity. On learning that he was Arjuna, the Pandava prince, the King told him that one of his ancestors in the kingly line, named Prabhanjana, was childless for quite a long time. In order to obtain a successor he performed severe penances. Lord Shiva who was pleased with his austerities, granted him a boon that he and his successors would each have one child. It so happened that the promised child had invariably been a son. But Chitravahana, was an exception, as he was the first to have only a daughter to continue his race whom he named as Chitrangada. He, therefore, treated her always as a son and had also made her his successor. The son that would be born to her would continue the race of the king. He demanded from Arjuna the son as the price of the marriage. On this consideration Arjuna could take her in marriage. Arjuna made a pledge to the King that the son born of this union would continue Chitravahana's race and then Arjuna took Chitrangada as his wife. He lived in her father's capital for three years. When a son was born to them, he embraced his wife with warmth, and bidding farewell to her and her father, set out again on his travels.

2.1. Tagore's *Chitra*

When the play opens we discover *Chitra* counselling with Madana, the god of Love, and Vasanta, the god of Spring and telling them how while wandering in pursuit of deer along the river bank she apprehends a man lying on a bed of leaves. The man referred to is Arjuna himself and she instantaneously feels aware for the first time in her life that she is a woman. She remembers that Arjuna has taken the vow of self-restraint and that she has always craved, in her mask as a male, to dare the Pandava warrior to single combat.

Chitra quickly gets rid of her man's semblance and hurries to Arjuna in the temple of Shiva. She appeals to the god of Spring to give her "but one brief day of perfect beauty"[2] and make her exquisitely beautiful, even as beautiful as the sudden flourishing of love in her heart. Her prayer is granted, and Arjuna is enamoured with love for Chitra by the charm, which the god of Love casts over him. When they at last meet, Chitra, tells Arjuna:

> Leave the little wild flower where it was born; leave it beautifully to die at the day's end among all the fading blossoms and the decaying leaves. Do not take it to your palace hall to fling it on the stony floor which knows no pity for things that fade and are forgotten.[3]

However Arjuna responds:

> Is ours that kind of love?

And Chitra softly answers back:

> Yes, no other. Why regret it? That which was meant for idle days should never outlive them. Joy turns into

> pain when the door by which it should depart is shut against it. Take it and keep it as long as it lasts. Let not the satiety of your evening claim more than the desire of your morning could earn... The day is done. Put this garland on. I am tired. Take me in your arms, my love. Let all vain bickerings of discontent die away at the sweet meeting of our lips.[4]

The twilight steals on the quiet faces of the two lovers and the sound of the prayer bells from the distant village comes floating on the evening breeze.

When the time arrives for the lovers to disunite, they have no remorse, for life has given them all. And Chitra says:

> If I stand up straight and strong with the strength of a daring heart spurning the wiles and arts of twining weakness, if I hold my head high like a tall young mountain fir, no longer trailing in the dust like a liana shall I then appeal to man's eye? No, no, you could not endure it.[5]

Thus, Chitra candidly confesses what she is in actuality. She alights from the world of dreams, poetry and romance woven around her to the world of reality, whereby the delicate playthings of transient youth which she had cloaked around herself, now leave her. Arjuna never seems to comprehend her, as he considers her to be a goddess hidden within a golden icon on account of which he cannot touch her and pay her his homage in return for her priceless gifts. She advances with a false front towards Arjuna, her lover. But, shortly later, the time arrives when she throws off her ornaments and veils, and stands clothed in unsheathed dignity. She says:

> I am Chitra. No goddess to be worshipped, nor yet the object of common pity to be brushed aside like a moth with indifference.[6]

On the other hand, Arjuna is not in the least discontented as he senses the reality. So he implores Chitra, to forget what he said to her in the past, as he will be fully satisfied with the present, wherein each separate moment of beauty comes to him like a bird of mystery from its unseen nest in the dark, bearing a message of music. He sees in Chitra, in spite of her blemishes, an image of nobility and grandeur, and says:

> Beloved, my life is full.[7]

Briefly speaking, Chitra first comes into view as an Atlanta, but when she sees Arjuna, the ascetic, the warrior becomes a woman. She must win his love, even on false pretences. The god of Love and the god of Spring give her heavenly beauty for the space of one year. Arjuna forgets his vows and surrenders to love. But each loves only the falsity in the other. Chitra's beauty is but obtained physical beauty and Arjuna's is a flawed gallant who has surged as a result of this assault of falsity. Neither is inwardly happy; she is unhappy because he does not really love her, and he is unhappy, because he senses that there is something wrong somewhere and he is, besides covertly drawn to the Chitra, the arms-bearer, the whip of her country's enemies. Yet in the end when the truth is forced out, real love sparks up from the ashes of the false love that has gone up in a blaze. Now love is born of deep understanding and shared experience, and this ultimately leads to the vision of their being true to their discarded selves. What the god of Spring foretold comes true:

> A time will come of itself when the heat-cloyed bloom of the body will droop and Arjuna will gladly accept the abiding fruitful truth in thee.[8]

Thus, Tagore's Chitra is the *essence of romance.* In the entire play the dialogues are full of passion, and they light up the way from Truth to Illusion and vice versa. Arjuna, vaguely glimpsing the truth but greatly confused still, says:

> I never seem to know you aright. You seem to me like a goddess hidden within a golden image. I cannot touch you, I cannot pay you my dues in return for your priceless gifts. Thus my love is incomplete. Sometimes in the enigmatic depth of your sad look, in your playful words mocking at their own meaning I gain glimpses of a being trying to rend asunder the languorous grace of her body, to emerge in a chaste fire of pain through a vaporous veil of smiles. Illusion is the first appearance of Truth. She advances towards her lover in disguise. But a time comes when she throws off her ornaments

> and veils and stands clothed in naked dignity. I grope for that ultimate you, that bare simplicity of truth.[9]

(i) The Theme

Tagore's representation of human love finds a beautiful exposition in *Chitra*. Tagore is both an idealist and a realist. He accepts the physical attraction between man and woman as true. It is equally true that if love is centred on the body and cannot impinge it, it degenerates into lust. The physical relationship between man and woman is the groundwork of love and the spiritual relation between them is its composition and the structure of love would remain incomplete without this composition. Love finds its attainment when the mind and the heart of the lover are in synchronicity with the mind and the heart of the beloved. Arjuna stands for the average man and Chitra for the average woman. Love between man and woman has a corporal basis. The attainment of love in *Chitra* takes place in the last scene of the play when Arjuna meets the real Chitra with all her physical imperfections and exclaims in delight, that his life is satiated.

The play is not designed to convey the meaning that sexual wantonness is an act of adoration. This is clear from the beginning when Arjuna offers his love to Chitra and is ready to break his vow of celibacy for the sake of love. Chitra is not thrilled with joy. On the other hand she says:

> Whom do you seek in these dark eyes, in these milk-white arms, if you are ready to pay for her the price of your probity? Not my true self, I know. Surely this cannot be love, this is not man's highest homage to woman! Alas, that this frail disguise, the body, should make one blind to the light of the deathless spirit! Yes, now indeed, I know, Arjuna, the fame of your heroic manhood is false.[10]

This passage conceives the body as the disguise and that the real self of a woman becomes gradually stronger. Then Chitra speaks to Arjuna:

> Would it please your heroic soul if the playmate of the night aspired to be the helpmeet of the day, if the left arm learnt to share the burden of the proud right arm?[11]

In reply Arjuna states his apprehension to know the real self of Chitra in the following words:

> I cannot touch you, I cannot pay you my dues in return for your priceless gifts. Thus my love is incomplete [...]. Illusion is the first appearance of Truth.[12]

Consequently, he lovingly accepts Chitra in her original form. And when they are about to part there is a feeling of attained maturity, experienced satisfaction and understanding.

In essence, the theme of *Chitra* is the evolution of human love. This idea is best illustrated in the words of K.R.S. Iyengar:

> Beauty and youth, although they may be transient, are yet a part of our experience. Wisdom lies in neither looking upon the body and its beauty as ends in themselves, nor in imagining that our life could wholly be separated from the physical base. Tagore rejected both 'negations'—the ascetic's denial of life as well as the sensualist's denial of the spirit. The blinding maddening ecstasy of the physical union is not denied in *Chitra* but its transience is also recognized. Even as illusion is but "the first appearance of truth" the fever and the throb of the senses are but a prelude to the less evanescent more subdued, joy of 'holy wedded love.'[13]

(ii) Chitra's Character

Tagore is an inheritor of the great literary tradition of Bengal, which regarded a woman as the primordial energy of the universe. Tagore's heroines belong to two broad categories, the type of feminine charm and the type of feminine grace, serene in her self-assurance and radiating a tranquil charm and silent power over the human heart. One is Urvashi and the other Lakshmi. Tagore's women characters display remarkable vivacity and dazzling variety. He considers the aura of dream surrounding many of the women characters as not merely the creation of God but also of man. They are not abstract entities, but creations of flesh and blood, pulsating with convincing liveliness. In his works women appear as mother, sister, daughter, wife, beloved, *Prakriti* in search of *Purusa,* and woman symbolizing the *Jivaatma,* who seeks union with the *Parmaatma.* There are also mythical, historical, religious, social, realistic and romantic characters, placed in several of his dramas, short stories and novels. He represents them as facing typical Indian problems and he explores deep into their hearts, with his keen psychological insight. His women characters are dynamic and are not the products of mere artistic control or manipulation.

Tagore's heroines are both feminine and unfeminine. They belong to the earth but they undergo tremendous changes in their encounter with harsh reality. Sometimes the two types—the emotional and the tranquilizing get fused as in *Chitra.* The diverse types of his women are basically human. They are enthroned as queens of the house, full of self-respect and self-confidence, exhibiting various moods.

There is an evolution in the character of Chitra which can be traced from dream to reality and the transition from the fire of flowery spring to the mellow fruitfulness of autumn. We find in her, as in Kalidasa's *Abhigyanshakuntalam,* the flowers of spring and the fruits of autumn. She advances from the paradise of sensual rapture to the ecstasy of illumination and the sustaining delight of wisdom. She has certainly lost one paradise, but she has gained another, which is the real paradise where woman holds undisputed sovereignty as a devoted wife and mother.

Chitra is the princess of Manipur. She is brought up as a warrior. When she glances at Arjuna in his ascetic robes for the first time, she becomes conscious of the fact or reality of her being a woman. She considers that she is beautiful enough to win his heart. She woos Arjuna but in vain, for he rejects her on the ground of his vow of celibacy. She does not abandon her love for she is not the kind of woman who nourishes her despair in lonely silence feeding it with nightly tears and covering it with the daily patient smile. In fact, Tagore has pointed out that the flower of her desire refuses to droop before it has been ripened into a fruit. She finds:

> it is the labour of a life-time to make one's true self fully known and honoured.[14]

She consequently chooses the easy path of illusion, *i.e.*, the acquired dazzle of beauty bestowed on her by the gods, Madana (god of Love) and Vasanta (god of Spring). In this role she fascinates and wins the heart of Arjuna who kneels down at Chitra's feet and begs for her love. He says:

> You alone are perfect; you are the wealth of the world, the end of all poverty, the goal of all efforts, the one woman![15]

From this point in the drama, we tread on the path of transition as Chitra through experience makes an effort to obtain self-knowledge. Gradually she realizes:

> Surely, this cannot be love, this is not man's highest homage to woman! Alas that this frail disguise, the body, should make one blind to the light of the deathless spirit![16]

Again she says:

> Woo not falsehood, offer not your great heart to an illusion. Go.[17]

Thus, with the progress of time Chitra's practical experiences instruct her into self-knowledge.

Chitra is fully conscious that her procured beauty would shortly vanish, as the petals fall from an overblown flower, the only moment of her sweet union would slip from her, leaving her ashamed of her exposed poverty, which she will spend weeping day and night. It is impossible for her to keep her disguise and she prefers to accept the hard truth sooner than the false happiness.

There is another aspect of Chitra's personality as a terror of evil doers and as father and mother to her people. It lies in the fact of her being a brave girl. She is a man in valour, but all woman in tenderness. Arjuna thinks of her as the goddess of Victory:

> Like a watchful lioness she protects the litter at her dugs with a fierce love. Woman's arms though adorned with nought, but unfettered strength, are beautiful! My heart is restless, fair one, like a serpent, reviving from his long winter's sleep. Come, let us both race on swift horses side by side, like twin orbs of light sweeping through space.[18]

Chitra seems to him like a goddess hidden within a golden image, notwithstanding what she is beneath the disguise. The flowers of Spring have already matured into the mellow fruits of autumn and the bell for them to part has rung. The day when they would part arrives. The illusion is shattered and Chitra, the playmate of Arjuna's night, appears as the helpmate of the day showing her true self. Chitra says:

> The gift that I proudly bring you is the heart of a woman. Here have all pains and joys gathered, the hopes and fears and shames of a daughter of the dust; Here love springs up struggling towards immortal life. Herein lies an imperfection which yet is noble and grand. If the flower-service is finished, my master, accept this as your servant for the days to come![19]

Thus before parting from Chitra, Arjuna accepts her in bliss when she casts on him a tranquilizing spell. Chitra becomes all the more beautiful because she has known love, and because she is now a prospective mother.

(iii) Symbolism in *Chitra*

In *Chitra,* symbolism plays an important role. It is based on the well-known *Mahabharata* story of Chitrangada and Arjuna. *Chitra* essentially contains the history of a development—the development of flower into fruit, of earth into heaven, of matter into spirit.

There are two unions in *Chitra.* The first union takes place in the second scene. And the next union takes place in the ninth scene of the play. This play was not meant for dealing with a particular passion but for translating the whole subject from one world to another—to elevate love from the sphere of physical beauty to the eternal heaven of moral beauty.

The central symbol in *Chitra* is the offer of beauty to Chitra by the gods, Madana and Vasanta, for the span of a year. The symbol is not deliberately exhibited, it grows naturally and spontaneously out of the story. Chitra has been brought up as a son by her father. She falls in love with Arjuna, who however does not reciprocate her love. He on the contrary says:

> I have taken the vow of celibacy. I am not fit to be thy husband.[20]

Nonetheless, Chitra feels desperate on being scorned like this and seeks the help of the gods, Madana and Vasanta, to whom she says:

> Had I but the time needed, I could win his heart by slow degrees, and ask no help of the gods.[21]

She also states:

> But it is the labour of a life time to make one's true self known and honoured.[22]

But, she is prompted by her desire to be immediately satisfied. She, therefore, requests to the gods:

> For a single day make me superbly beautiful, even as beautiful as was the sudden blooming of love in my heart. Give me but one brief day of perfect beauty, and I will answer for the days that follow.[23]

Her prayer is granted with a significant qualification:

> Not for the short span of a day, but for one whole year the charm of spring blossoms shall nestle round thy limbs.[24]

On this being accepted, the action moves on in a poetic-realistic mood, and presents a spectacle of Arjuna's obsession; their living together in perfect bliss; Arjuna's boredom and his longing for the other, real Chitra; the falling off of Chitra's mask of beauty at the end of the year; Arjuna's happy and proud acceptance of the real Chitra and the final spiritual fulfilment. There is no conflict between the surface-realistic level and the deeper symbolic meaning. The symbolic meaning is related to the essential duality of life, which in the story expresses itself as the duality of love. There is no contradiction between Infinite and Finite, Truth and Illusion, Spirit and Body, Love and Desire, Joy and Pain, Peace and Restlessness, True self and False self, but what is most remarkable in the play is that the latter *i.e.*, Finite, Illusion, Body, Desire, Pain, Restlessness, False self are transmitted into the former *i.e.*, Infinite, Truth, Spirit, Love, Joy, Peace, and True self. This transformation occurs primarily because of Time, which plays, a crucial part in the entire play.

The time factor plays a significant part in the form of the gods' offer of beauty to Chitra for a year. This central symbol fully and organically set in the play is assisted by the symbolic gods, Madana, the body-less god of abiding love and Vasanta, the time-bound god of spring. The symbol is assisted by images of flower and fruit and by the image of flame, which symbolizes the upward, restless, and burning process of love.

In short, Chitra stands for human desire; Arjuna stands as the seeker of love; the gods Madana and Vasanta stand for love and youth and beauty respectively.

The symbols in *Chitra* are an organic part of the theme. *Chitra* combines the flowers of spring with the fruits of autumn. It also combines heaven and earth. Truly, in *Chitra* there is one Paradise Lost and another Paradise Regained.

2.2. Variations in Tagore's *Chitra*

Like Shakespeare, Kalidas, and Shelley, Tagore deviated from the original story to suit his requirements. The following are the variations that are observed in the text of Tagore from the *Mahabharata:*

1. The Chitrangada-Arjuna episode in the *Mahabharata* runs up to 15 verses, (beginning from stanza no. 13 to stanza no. 27), while Tagore's drama involves nine scenes.
2. In the *Mahabharata*, Arjuna meets Chitravahana, the King of Manipur, whereas in Tagore's *Chitra*, Arjuna never encounters the King.
3. In the *Mahabharata*, Arjuna accidently meets Chitrangada while in Tagore's *Chitra*, it is Chitra who sees Arjuna accidently.
4. In the *Mahabharata*, Chitrangada has been depicted as a youthful damsel of exquisite beauty. She is *Charudarsana* and *Vararoha*, whereas in Tagore's *Chitra*, Chitra is unattractive and plain. The whole plot of the drama hinges on this point. Had Chitra been a beautiful woman she would not have approached Madana (Eros) and Vasanta (Lycoris) for lending her charm and grace even for a day, so that she might win the heart of Arjuna.
5. In the *Mahabharata*, Arjuna makes up his mind to have Chitrangada as his wife and therefore he goes to the

King and seeks his permission for the hand of Chitrangada, whereas in Tagore's *Chitra*, Arjuna does not seek her hand in marriage with the permission of her father or any of her guardians.

6. In the *Mahabharata*, Arjuna lives with Chitrangada in Manipur for three years, while in Tagore's *Chitra*, Arjuna stays with her for only a year.
7. In the *Mahabharata*, Chitrangada gives birth to a boy-child and Arjuna leaves after having presented the son to the father of Chitrangada, whereas in Tagore's *Chitra*, Arjuna is illuminated with revelation after a year and is reminded of his home. Here Chitra offers the last sacrifice at Arjuna's feet (*i.e.*, flowers of incomparable beauty from the garden of heaven and tells Arjuna that she will teach her child to be a second Arjuna).
8. In the *Mahabharata*, Chitrangada is observed as a submissive daughter and wife. She accepts anything and everything, while in Tagore's *Chitra*, Chitra is a strong-willed daughter and a fierce individual.

2.3. The *Savitri* Legend

Savitrya preetaya datta Savitrya hutaya hyapi
Savitrityeva namasyaschakrurvipraastatha pita.[25]

Savitri is based on the *Mahabharata* legend of Savitri and Satyavan. Aswapathi, the king of the Madra kingdom was a popular king, but his one worry was that he had no child. So he performed austerities for eighteen years. The goddess Savitri, then appeared and vouchsafed the boon of a daughter of great beauty.

As prophesized by the goddess, the queen gave birth to a female child before the end of the year. The child was named Savitri, who grew up to be an intelligent, courageous and beautiful girl. She was loved by all in the kingdom.

The King then told Savitri to choose her life partner, a prince who would be worthy of her. In obedience with the royal command, Savitri travelled with an escort, visiting many countries, till finally she chose Prince Satyavan who was living in a forest hermitage with his father, the blind king

Dyumathsena of the Shalwas and mother Shaibya who had lost their kingdom.

Savitri returned home, jubilant and satisfied with her choice, She found her father with the famous sage Narada, who immediately asked her who she had chosen for her husband. When Narada heard that Satyavan was her choice, he begged Savitri to reconsider her decision, as he knew that Satyavan had only one more year to live. But she was determined to marry Satyavan, with whom she was already deeply in love. And so, ignoring the pleas and appeals of her family, she married Satyavan at Dyumathsena's hermitage in a simple ceremony. Savitri and Satyavan went round the sacred fire hand in hand as the priests chanted Vedic mantras.

Savitri and Satyavan loved each other, and were happy together. However, she carried a heavy heart, as she could not forget the prophecy regarding Satyavan's life. Time flew by. Savitri realised that Satyavan's death was approaching. Four days prior to the prophesized end of Satyavan, Savitri undertook a *Tri-Ratra* vow. On the day marked for Satyavan's death, he set out to the woods with an axe upon his shoulders as usual. Savitri begged him to allow her to accompany him, and with the permission of the in-laws they walked into the forest.

As he was chopping wood, Satyavan felt some pain. He rested his head on Savitri's lap and fell into a slumber. Nearby, a dark shadowy figure emerged, carrying a noose in his hand. He was Yama, the god of Death. Masking her fear of the god, Savitri pleaded with him not to take her husband from her, but Yama refused to listen and started carrying Satyavan away. Savitri followed, persistent and unyielding, as Yama traversed through the forests with Satyavan on his shoulder. Savitri pleased him with her discourse and purity of heart. Yama then told her to ask for any boon except for her husband's life.

Being wise, Savitri immediately asked that her father-in-law's eyesight should be restored. The boon was granted, but Savitri did not leave. Yama then granted her three more boons. As a second boon, Savitri asked for the restoration of Dyumathsena's kingdom. This was granted. Her third boon demanded that her own father be blessed with a hundred sons. This too was granted. As the fourth boon, she asked that she herself should bear a hundred sons. Yama granted this boon too, not recognizing the predicament he was to face. Savitri smiled, pointing out to Yama that she could not have a hundred sons without her husband being restored to life. Realising that he had been outwitted, Yama released the soul of Satyavan from his noose.

Savitri returned to the place where Satyavan's body lay. She took his head on her lap, and within a moment, Satyavan regained his life. The couple then proceeded back to Dyumathsena. Concluding his narrative, Rishi Markandeya said:

> Even thus did Savitri redeem from peril and raise to high fortune herself, her father and mother, her father-in-law, as also the whole race of her husband.[26]

2.4. Aurobindo's *Savitri*

In the story narrated by Aurobindo, Savitri and Satyavan acquire a symbolic significance. Savitri stands for the true wife's constant power of devotion and divine grace, and Satyavan stands for divine truth. Aurobindo, according to the age-old epic tradition plunges into the middle of the story, and the earlier parts are narrated at a later stage.

The First Book (The Book of Beginnings) opens on the day Satyavan must die. Already twelve passionate months have elapsed since the marriage of Savitri and Satyavan, and the fatal day has dawned. But the day is also the symbol dawn of a new epoch in cosmic history. There is thus double time in *Savitri*. Like the double time, there is double-action also: on the material plane the poem begins on the day Satyavan is fated to die, and the poem ends with the embarrassment of Yama, the Lord of Death and the return of Satyavan to life. On the spiritual plane, the poem plunges into the middle of the action—the fateful hour in human history when the *Aasuric* creation (the evil) threatens the world and all the great achievements of the race with total extinction. This issue between threatening Death and the hope of New Life is unfolded in *Savitri*. Savitri wakes up in her forest hermitage at dawn and ponders over the fateful 'issue' to be faced. In her sublime solitariness and self-possession she appears a victoress, a world-saviour. Who is this Savitri, why is she here, how has the issue been joined? Aurobindo takes us back to the days of King Ashwapathy's austerities, his prolonged yoga when he yearned for a child.

Even as Savitri's predicament on the fatal day is presented, her special status, her divine origin too is stressed. The day has dawned as other days to all except Savitri; only she knows the encounter ahead, the battle that must be fought and won before the following dawn. Satyavan's nearing death is a link in an endless chain of thwarted purposings in this foul and imperfect earth. And it is the burden of Savitri's destiny:

> To wrestle with the Shadow she had come
> And must confront the riddle of man's birth
> And life's brief struggle in dumb Matter's night.[27]

She is Savitri, the anxious agonized wife, bearing the weight of an intolerable and frightful inevitability; but she is the great world Mother. The human and the divine are locked in her in an intimate, unutterable embrace. Hence, she faces the future with strong will-power and also with a deep tranquillity and self-mastery:

> Whether to bear with Ignorance and Death
> Or hew the ways of Immortality,
> To win or lose the godlike game for man,
> Was her soul's issue thrown with Destiny's dice
> But not to submit and suffer was she born;
> To lead, to deliver was her glorious part.[28]

The remaining three cantos of Book I and Book II (The Book of the Traveller of the Worlds) and Book III (The Book of the Divine Mother) take the action backwards and tell us about the yoga of King Aswapathy. He descends to the worlds below mapped out in psychic terms: the worlds of gross matter, subtle matter, little life (insect, animal, early man) and greater life (the heroic age) which achieves Power yet invites or permits corruption. The further step below is hell: the all-too-familiar World of Falsehood, the Mother of Evil, and the Sons of Darkness. But even Hell is the Eternal's shadowy veil. With this realisation that injects hope in him when all seemed hopeless, Ashwapathy ascends to the Worlds of the Gandharvas, and of the Little Mind, and the Greater Mind; to the Paradisal Heavens of the Ideal; to the Centre of Silence within, where he gains an insight into the *Purusha-Prakriti* origin of the cosmos; and behind the eternal twain, the soul of the omnipotent Goddess ever-veiled, whose mask is the making of the world and whose footfalls are the rages of the ages. He is the aspiring human soul in his search for the truth of himself, of the world, and of God.

The description of Aswapathy's Yoga takes up about 370 pages, while the second Book (spread over 15 cantos) extends to nearly 250 pages. Finally, Aswapathy aspires no longer for himself but for all, for a universal realization and a new creation. That is described in Book III (The Book of the Divine Mother). He carries to the Divine Mother the intense aspiration of the earth and as its representative prays to Her to come down to the earth and his prayer is granted by the Divine Mother:

> A seed shall be sown in Death's tremendous hour,
> A branch of heaven transplant to human soil;
> Nature shall over-leap her mortal step;
> Fate shall be changed by an unchanging will.[29]

The Fourth Book (The Book of Birth and Quest) brings the reader to the worldly drama of the epic. The fulfilment of the Divine Mother's boon to the King begins here. The first canto describes the birth and childhood of Savitri; the second details the ideal, harmonious atmosphere of Madra, the kingdom of Aswapathy where Savitri grows up; in the third canto Aswapathy asks Savitri to venture through the deep world to find her life-mate and the fourth canto narrates the quest of Savitri for her mate.

The Fifth Book (The Book of Love) deals with the meeting of Savitri and Satyavan. Her wandering feet leads her to the hermitage where young Satyavan is in attendance on his blind aged father, King Dyumathsena and his Queen Shaibya now deprived of their throne. Savitri and Satyavan meet in sudden felicity and recognize the hand of fate:

> Thus, were they in each other lost awhile,
> Then drawing back from their long ecstasy's trance

Came into a new self and a new world
Each now was a part of the other's unity.[30]

The Sixth Book (The Book of Fate) deals with the sequel to this love. Returning to her father, Savitri is about to report her joy. Her face is transfigured by happiness and Narad himself, the divine Sage, thrilled with wonder asks:

He cried to her, 'Who is this that comes, the bride,
The flame-born, and round her illumined head
Pouring their lights her hymeneal pomps
Move flashing about her?
From what green glimmer of glades
Retreating into dewy silences
Or half-seen verge of waters moon-betrayed
Bringst though this glory of enchanted eyes?'[31]

Savitri now speaks about Satyavan, and Narad feels dejected. When questioned he praises Satyavan's manifold perfections but adds that he is fated to die a year hence. Savitri, however, is undismayed:

Once my heart chose and chooses not again.
The word I have spoken can never be erased,
It is written in the record book of God [...]
Death's grip can break our bodies, not our souls;
If death take him, I too know how to die
Let Fate do with me what she will or can;
I am stronger than Death and greater than my fate;
My love shall outlast the world, doom falls from me
Helpless against my immortality.
Fate's law may change but not my spirit's will.[32]

Her mother's worldly wisdom also fails to affect Savitri's decision. Savitri knows that Death can be met and chased away. Narad also sees wondrous power possibilities being realized as the result of Savitri's willpower. So he assures Aswapathy and Queen Shaibya that all will be well and that Savitri is cast for a uniquely cosmic role of struggle and redemption. They must not interfere with the working of Destiny:

A day may come when she must stand unhelped
On a dangerous brink of the world's doom and hers,

Carrying the world's future on her lonely breast,
Carrying the human hope in a heart left sole
To conquer or fail on a last desperate verge.
Alone with death and close to extinction's edge,
Her single greatness in that last dire scene.
She must cross alone a perilous bridge in Time
And reach an apex of world-destiny
Where all is won or all is lost for man.[33]

The Seventh Book (The Book of Yoga) begins with a description of the wedded love of Satyavan and Savitri. But the joy of the union is marred by her foreknowledge of Satyavan's approaching death and the consequent ache in her heart. Savitri, the incarnation of the Divine Mother, is nevertheless a limited human being in appearance; her surface human reactions however do not belie the veiled divinity in her heart. She is the golden fruit of Aswapathy's Yoga and she herself becomes a Yogin, determined to know herself fully and realize her strength, and to be in readiness for the coming trial. And therefore she tries to prepare herself in order to change the decree of Fate regarding Satyavan. As she begins an inner search for her soul's identity and seeks her inner soul, the realization comes to her that the Divine Mother has made her. The darkness threatening her life with Satyavan being sympomatic of the present human predicament, she would track it to its source and master and transform it. In the spiritual and psychological realms within her, she comes across several possibilities—the triple soul-forces—but it is the total power of the Soul that is the need of the hour. She gains this by achieving a great calm, the Superconscient's high retreat, and is now ready for the great struggle.

The Eighth Book (The Book of Death) gives an account of the death of Satyavan on the fated day. As Satyavan walks beside Savitri while going to the forest, she keeps herself composed and silent. But her heart is heavy. Reaching the forest, Satyavan starts collecting fuel. Soon Death approaches him. He feels a piercing pain in his head, and cries to Savitri:

And he cried to her, 'Savitri a pang
Cleaves through my head and breast as if the axe
Were piercing it and not the living branch.
Such agony rends me as the tree must feel

When it is sundered and must lose its life
Awhile let me lay head upon thy lap
And guard me with thy hands from evil fate:
Perhaps because thou touchest, death may pass.'[34]

He lays his head upon her lap and urges her to guard him from evil fate. He expresses the hope that Death may pass because she touches him. She tries to soothe his anguished brow and body with her hands. Presently, he calls her thrice and dies. She now feels the presence of someone near her. It is Death in visible form.

The next three Books (IX-The Book of Eternal Night, X-The Book of the Double Twilight, and XI-The Book of Everlasting Day) give a detailed account of the delayed struggle between Savitri and Yama for the soul of Satyavan. Savitri's ordeal takes her through the symbol world of eternal night with its oppressive load of evil, pain, death and the double twilight. Every argument made, every persuasion offered, to Savitri to make her give up her demand for the restoration of Satyavan's life, is argued firmly or rejected resolutely. But this Savitri, has the daring to stand up to Death. When Yama questions:

Wilt thou for ever keep thy passionate hold,
Thyself a creature doomed like him to pass,.
Denying his soul death's calm and silent rest?
Relax thy grasp; this body is earth's and thine,
His spirit now belongs to a greater power.[35]

Savitri replies:

I will bear with him the ancient Mother's load,
I will follow with him earth's path that leads to God [...]
Wherever thou leadst his soul I shall pursue.[36]

Death speaks in terms of worldly wisdom but she firmly holds on to love. Death's sophistries are in vain for Savitri will not be deceived. She says:

O Death, who reasonest, I reason not,
Reason that scans and breds, but cannot build
Or builds in vain because she doubts her work.
I am, I love, I see, I act, I will.[37]

Savitri has now no option but to assume her cosmic form, to

appear in her true divine self. This is the supreme moment in the spiritual action of the epic when Love faces Death. Savitri, the personification of Love states:

> My will is greater than thy law, O Death;
> My love is stronger than the bonds of Fate:
> Our love is the heavenly seal of the supreme.
> I guard that seal against thy rending hands.[38]

To this, Death firmly remarks:

> In me all take refuge, for I, Death, am God.[39]

But Savitri is resolute. She replies:

> My heart is wiser than the Reason's thoughts,
> My heart is stronger than thy bonds, O Death [...]
> ... ...
> Nothing I claim but Satyavan alone.[40]

Death finds himself suddenly helpless as his associates, Night, Hell and the Inconscient, desert him. The light that overpowers and transforms everything eats up his body. Satyavan is no doubt won back, however, for Savitri herself, the trial is not yet over. She has still to face the temptations. She contemplates whether they should return to the earth or not? Shouldn't they enjoy paradisal felicity forever? Why not opt for *Nirvana*? But Savitri is not to be deflected from her purpose. She will not accept personal salvation. Rather she will with Satyavan at her side, return to the earth, and 'build there' the bliss of Heaven.

The Twelfth Book (Epilogue) tells us of the defeat of Death; the coming back of Satyavan to life; the return of Savitri and Satyavan to the earth; and the beginning of the task of divinising earth life by Savitri and Satyavan.

(i) The Theme

Love along with the evolution of the human soul is a major motif in *Savitri*. Herein the love and fidelity of a *pativrata* wife conquers Death itself. It shows the power of love, the grandeur and vastness it imparts to the human soul and also how it enables the human to overcome all obstacles in the way. Savitri is divinised by her love. There is in her a human will, an innate tendency, and an inborn capacity for disinterested love. This power to love others is one of the things that make human beings like God. Needless to say that every Indian knows Savitri's debate with Death, and her ultimate triumph over mortality.

In Aurobindo's *Savitri* the *Mahabharata* story is raised to the level of a cosmic drama, being played out as much on earth as in the realms of the eternal. And Savitri's love is not for Satyavan alone, and her fight is not for the life of her husband alone, but her personal story has been universalized and her personal trouble and struggle is shown to be but the sign and symbol of the sweat of mankind. Savitri, as presented in the epic is the eternal feminine, the great World Mother.

Savitri is primarily a poem of love and Aurobindo a poet of love. This is true not only of Book V, called *The Book of Love*, but of the poem as a whole. The poet states:

> There is a power within that knows beyond
> Our knowings; we are greater than our thoughts,
> And sometimes earth unveils that vision here.
> To live, to love are signs of infinite things,
> Love is a glory from eternity's spheres.
> Abased, disfigured, mocked by baser mights
> That steal his name and shape and ecstasy,
> He is still the Godhead by which all can change.[41]

Savitri is determined to change the fate of man. She is bold and fearless as observed in her discussion with her father. She says:

> Death's grip can break our bodies, not our souls;
> If death take him, I too know how to die.
> Let Fate do with me what she will or can;
> I am stronger than death and greater than my fate;
> My love shall outlast the world, doom falls from me
> Helpless against my immortality,
> Fate's law may change, but not my spirit's will.[42]

She further adds:

> I shall walk with him like gods in Paradise.
> If for a year that year is all my life
> And yet I know this is not all my fate
> Only to live and love awhile and die.
> For I know now why my spirit came on earth
> And who I am and who he is I love.[43]

Savitri knows the power of love. She encounters the Lord of Death with her great words:

> O Death, who reasonest, I reason not,
> Reason that scans and breaks, but cannot build
> Or builds in vein because she doubts her work
> I am, I love, I see, I act. I will.[44]

Savitri tells the god of Death:

> My love is not a hunger of the heart,
> My love is not a craving of the flesh;
> It came to me from God, to God returns.[45]

Savitri may truly be called celebration of the glory, the greatness and the power of love. The heroine Savitri struggles to make Satyavan—and all mankind—eternal and, therefore, she explains to Yama the outstanding significance of love:

> My love is stronger than the bonds of Fate.
> Our love is the heavenly seal of the Supreme.
> I guard that seal against thy rending hands.
> Love must not cease to live upon the earth;
> For Love is the bright link twixt earth and heaven,
> Love is the far Transcendent's angel here;
> Love is man's lien on the Absolute.[46]

Savitri succeeds in saving her husband from the noose of Death and finally a sage asks her to explain the miracle. She then replies:

> Awakened to the meaning of my heart,
> That to feel love and oneness is to live
> And this the magic of our golden change
> Is all the truth I know or seek, O sage.[47]

Thomas Kempis rightly states on parallel lines:

> Love is a mighty power, a great and complete good. Love alone lightens every burden, and makes the rough places smooth [...]. Nothing is sweeter than love, nothing stronger, nothing higher, nothing wider, nothing more pleasant, nothing fuller or better in heaven or earth for love is born of God, and can rest only in God, above all created things.[48]

Thus, in *Savitri* all the chief characters are redeemed by

love. The type of love here is not love, which implies acquiescence with evil. Great and true love is a power that can break the doors of captivity and can transform the superfluous, the unused into something precious and can even defy death.

(ii) Savitri's Character

Savitri is a powerful woman character of the legend of Savitri and Satyavan, taken from the *Mahabharata*. Aurobindo has considerably enriched and glorified her character. Savitri, in the legend is the very model of a chaste and loyal wife, who can face even death for the sake of her husband.

Savitri is born to king Aswapathy as a result of a boon granted to him by the goddess Savitri, the World-Mother. She is brought up in beautiful nature-surroundings, and therefore she imbibes the dignity and majesty of nature herself. She grows up into a radiant, dignified, intelligent and beautiful young lady. Her radiant beauty also strikes Narad too. He states:

> Who is this that comes, the bride,
> The flame-born, and round her illumined head,
> Pouring their lights, hymeneal pomps
> Move flashing about her?
> From what green glimmer of glades
> Retreating into dewy silences
> Or half-seen verge of waters moon-betrayed
> Brings thou this glory of enchanted eyes?[49]

As exclusively seen by Ashwapathy, by Narad and by her fellow-ashramites, Savitri is both goddess-like and lovable and unmistakably human. Following her father's order she starts her quest and at last she meets Satyavan in the forest and falls deeply in love with him. Inspite of her parent's disapproval on account of the short life span of Satyavan, she firmly resolves to marry Satyavan and Satyavan alone. This throws light on the extraordinary willpower of Savitri. She says:

> My will is part of the eternal will,
> My fate is what my spirit's strength can make,
> My fate is what my spirit's strength can bear;
> My strength is not the titan's, it is God's.[50]

Similarly, Henry David Thoreau in his *Journal* (1854) talks about every human being as being the artificer of his/her own fate. As such, events, circumstances have their origin in ourselves. They spring from seeds, which we have sown.

Savitri marries Satyavan. She knows about her future but at the same time she is determined to change her destined situation. But she tells her woe to none, she suffers silently, and gathers all her spiritual resources to save the life of Satyavan from the clutches of Death, and then to alter human destiny and nature's law. Her fight with death is not to be a fight for her own sake, but she rather regards her private fate as a sign and symbol of the fate of humanity. It is to be a fight with Death for the sake of humanity; she is determined to change human destiny and make Satyavan immortal. It is universal love, which inspires and moves her and she seeks to change Nature's law.

Savitri's personality has been heightened and magnified to epic dimensions. She is known to be a super-human being who stands firm and determined like a resistant figure, to face death and break the cosmic law of Karma.

Through her discussion with Yama, we come to know about various aspects of Savitri's personality. She says:

> My mind is a torch lit from the eternal sun,
> My life a breath drawn by the immortal Guest
> My mortal body is the Eternal's house.[51]

Again she says:

> I am not bound by thought or sense or shape;
> I live in the glory of the Infinite,
> I am near to the Nameless and Unknowable,
> The ineffable is now my household mate...
> But I have loved too the body of my God.
> I have pursued him in his earthly form.[52]

Savitri has accepted her birth:

> To wrestle with the Shadow she had come
> And must confront the riddle of man's birth
> And life's brief struggle in dumb Matter's night [...]
> Or hew the ways of Immortality,
> To win or loose the godlike game for man,

Was her soul's issue thrown with Destiny's dice
But not to submit and suffer was she born;
To lead, to deliver was her glorious part.[53]

Savitri does not accept the Karmic law which binds the present to the past. She can reverse the march of destiny and change the law of determinism.

Aurobindo's *Savitri* is the symbol of all that is great, heroic, and noble in Man. She symbolises the powers and energies of the spirit through which even the impossible can be achieved. She symbolizes the power of love, which raises the human to the level of the Divine.

In short, Savitri has beauty, strong willpower and capacity for love, which enables her to defy and master her fate.

(iii) Symbolism in *Savitri*

Aurobindo himself has entitled the epic *Savitri* as a legend and a symbol. Therefore its symbolic interpretation is much more significant in order to understand the epic. All the names have been used symbolically. Savitri is not merely an accomplished princess, but a being who embodies Divine Grace, the incarnation of goddess Usha, the Mother of eternal light, the great World-Mother, descended on earth, to work out the salvation of man, and change human destiny. She symbolises the Light of Wisdom that struggles with the Darkness of Ignorance symbolised by Yama, and overcomes it. Her struggle with Death for the life of Satyavan becomes symbolic of the aspiring human soul to break the chain of determinism—the eternal chain of *Karma,* which binds the present to the past—and thus establish life divine on earth. Satyavan symbolizes one who possesses truth or at least one who aspires for it. The union of Savitri and Satyavan is thus the union of Truth and Light—the light of knowledge, the light of wisdom, the light of the spirit—and together, they do overcome the Darkness and Ignorance of the material world and establish the kingdom of God on earth, where Truth prevails and the reign of darkness has no power.

Aswapathy, the name of the father of Savitri, means the Lord of Life, the symbol of life-energy or vital power. In the epic, he symbolizes the soul of Man aspiring for self-knowledge. The life of the childless king Aswapathy performing *tapasya* in order to have a child has been entirely changed by the poet into a symbol of human soul descended on earth from divine heights trying to acquire knowledge of the Self and the world. The entire Second Book is, in fact, Aswapathy's travel over worlds heaped upon worlds in a complex cosmogony mounting from the plinth of the plane of matter right up to levels of the Higher Mind and the plane of the Cosmic Being leading to worlds of greater knowledge.

Aswapathy represents the aspiring human soul in search of the Truth of himself, of the world and of God. He acquires by his *tapasya* immense knowledge of the possibilities of the human consciousness, its deeper depths and its highest heights. In his heart burns the flame of aspiration to create here on earth an image of perfection, which his soul feels is possible for man and earth to attain. But Aswapathy feels that unless the Divine Mother incarnates herself down on earth it would not be possible to create the world of Truth here (Life-Divine in the midst of life human). The supreme Mother in her infinite grace gives Aswapathy a boon that a human manifestation of her Grace would be born on earth. A new light shall break upon the earth, a New World shall be born, and things that were promised shall be fulfilled.

Aswapathy's penances symbolize the trials and tribulations of the evolving Soul of Humanity and his gains are the gains of the human race during its long struggle for attainment of the Truth. Savitri, throughout, the epic poem, is treated as one conscious of her Divinity and at the same time conscious of her humanity. The episode of Narad's declaration of the fate of Satyavan has been raised to a high pitch of spirituality wherein cosmic purposes and intentions, the destiny of man, are brought into play. In the original legend, as also in the symbol Savitri faces Yama, the god of Death. But in the legend the conversation which takes place between Savitri and Yama is rather conventional, but in the epic, Savitri clearly stands not merely as the representative of the race but also as the embodiment of the supreme Grace. Yama, on the other hand puts before her all the opposition with the subtlety, ingenuity and cunning that Ignorance can devise. The whole dialogue moves on a very high plane of inspiration in which brilliant flashes of revelation and over-mental lightening occasionally break forth. Here also one sees how the poet has enriched the original legend, how far in fact, he has heightened the Indian myth by turning it into a rich episode full of significance for the human soul and its destiny. He has turned a local legend into a tremendous psychological fact full of significance for human evolution. It is this transforming power which is the alchemy of the great master. K.R.S. Iyengar writes:

> Savitri is symbolic of the true wife's devotion and power—unflinching devotion and power—even to overcome the greatest of evils, Death. And Satyavan is Truth. Beauty, love and power (the power of devotion and chastity) allied to Truth can dare anything, achieve anything since Aurobindo's Yoga was a "world transforming Yoga," since it assumed the possibility of mind being transformed into 'supermind,' limited self-divided earth-nature being transcended by 'supernature' and earth-life by the life-divine, he chose as the fit symbol the hero and the heroine of his epic of the evolving soul, the immaculate Satyavan and Savitri, names already familiar to us, and charged with untold significance by association with the ancient Hindu scriptures and epics [...]. If Aswapathy is aspiration, Savitri is both the response and the resulting transformation—at once the individual transformation of an elected person and the promise of the total transformation of earth and earth-nature.[54]

Savitri reflects the destiny of the whole human species in the process of evolution. So, it may be said that Savitri traces symbolically the evolution of the Spirit from the Inconscient Matter, *Annamaya Kosha,* to the Superconscient Divine, the *Vigyanamaya Kosha.* In this respect, it may be noted that the spirit and the substance of Vedic poetry largely influence Savitri.

In short, Aswapathy, Dyumathsena, Yama, Satyavan and Savitri are the principal symbols of the epic. They are conventional symbols in the sense that their names signify those qualities, which they embody. The term Aswapathy is the combination of two words "*Aswa*" (Horse) and "*Pati*" (Lord). A horse means the "life-energy" in the Vedic sense of the term. Etymologically, Aswapathy, therefore would mean the Lord of life-energy. Aswapathy has controlled his Vital and Mental energy and liberated himself from Ignorance. So he can ascend to the higher and occult worlds of consciousness.

Dyumathsena is the symbol of the divine mind. He is said to be blind because he does not have the Divine Light (knowledge of God). And therefore he has lost his kingdom of bliss.

Yama, says the Veda is the binder, the restrainer. Restraining or binding is the feature of the lower nature. Divine consciousness is restricted and so it becomes Ignorance, which in terms of Aurobindo, is real Death. Death thus means the Ignorance, which separates us from knowledge, Power, Bliss, and Peace of the Divine.

Satyavan is one who is the seeker of Truth (Truth being God-Knowledge). He has seen glimpses of Truth and God in the phenomena; so his mind is liberated. But he does not know how to divinise his body. He has to die so that he can liberate his body from the pulls of inconscient matter. The Death of Satyavan thus becomes the symbol of earth's creation, of its fate and through Savitri, of its liberation. She faces the doom in order to give the solution.

Savitri stands for the creative power of the Sun. The word Savitri is derived from the root "*Su*" which means, "to give birth to." For the Vedic seers, Savitri is the Solar Power that creates, sustains and guides the universe. For Aurobindo, she is the incarnation of the Divine Grace who aims to liberate man from the clutches of Death and Fate. Indeed, Savitri is the Love of the Divine Mother that comes down to transmute Death and to hew the ways of immortality:

> For this she had accepted mortal breath;
> To wrestle with the Shadow she had come
> And must confront the riddle of man's birth
> And life's brief struggle in dumb Matter's night.[55]

Aurobindo explains the symbolic meanings of the different characters thus:

> Satyavan is the soul carrying the divine truth of being within itself but descended into the grip of death and ignorance; Savitri is the Divine Word, daughter of the

Sun, Goddess of the Supreme Truth, who comes down and is born to save; Ashwapathy, the lord of Horse, her human father, is the lord of Tapasya, the concentrated energy of the spiritual endeavour that helps us to rise from the mortal to the immortal planes; Dyumathsena, lord of the shining Hosts, father of Satyavan, is the divine Mind, here fallen blind losing its celestial kingdom of glory.[56]

2.5. Variations in Aurobindo's *Savitri*

The following are the deviations that are observed in the text of Aurobindo from the *Mahabharata*:

(i) In the legend, the character of Ashwapathy is described only in seven verses. He is said to have resorted to austerities for the personal gain of getting a child. But in *Savitri*, Aurobindo elaborates on the character of Ashwapathy in about twenty-three Cantos. He practices *yoga* not only for his own self-perfection but also for finding a way for man's liberation.

(ii) In the legend, the whole period of Ashwapathy's *tapasya* as reported has been transformed by the poet into an epic climb of the human soul in its journey from the inconscient to the very gates of the Superconscient.

(iii) In the legend, Savitri is said to be a gift of Goddess Savitri. But in the epic, the Divine Mother accepts the prayer of Ashwapathy and incarnates Herself as Savitri to vanquish Death.

(iv) The legend does not describe the growth of Savitri. But the epic narrates it in a Wordsworthian mode. It is said that Savitri grows imbibing the forces of Nature.

(v) The legend just mentions the meeting of Savitri and Satyavan. But the epic describes their meetings in detail for two reasons. First, it gives the poet an opportunity to sing the glory of love. Secondly, the poet can highlight the virtues of Satyavan. The meeting between Savitri and Satyavan is said to be the unique example of spiritual love.

(vi) In contrast to the legend, in the epic the episode of Narad's declaration of the fate of Satyavan has been raised to a very high pitch of spirituality where in cosmic purposes and intentions, the destiny of man, all are brought into play.

(vii) In the legend, the queen of Ashwapathy is merely a name. But in the epic, she is a very forceful character. She raises all those questions of life, which are usually asked by the agnostics to prove the non-existence of God. Narad patiently answers all her questions.

(viii) In the legend the conversation which takes place between Savitri and Yama is rather conventional, but in the epic, Savitri clearly stands not merely as the representative of the race but also as a representative of the Divine Mother. She defies the law of Death and defeats him with the strength of her divinity. Then Death is seen in a different form. A voice from infinity introduces him as the creator of the world and as the carrier of the seeds of thought. The whole dialogue moves on a very high plane of inspiration.

(ix) In the legend, Savitri and Satyavan, after the conquest of Death, return to the earth and Satyavan regains his father's kingdom and rules it for many years and is happy ever after with Savitri and their children. But in the poet's symbol both Savitri and Satyavan rise from the kingdom of Death to the region of the Eternal Day where the Sun of Truth never sets, where Ignorance is unknown and Death has no place. There she meets the Supreme Reality and asks for His Peace, Oneness, Energy and Joy for earthly creatures. After staying in this region of Truth for sometime, they look upon the earth and return to it in order to execute the Divine Will of raising human beings to the divine heights.

2.6. The Comparison between *Chitra* and *Savitri*

The points of Comparison are as follows:

(i) Both the works are inspired from the *Mahabharata*. *Chitra* forms a part of the Chitrangada-Arjuna episode in the *Adi Parva* of the *Mahabharata* whereas *Savitri* forms a part of the Savitri-Satyavan episode in the *Vana Parva* of the *Mahabharata*.

(ii) Both the works have been titled on the names of their heroines—Chitra and Savitri.

(iii) Both Chitra and Savitri are not puppets in the hands of the destiny. They are the creators and moulders of their own destiny.

(iv) In both the works the action takes place in the forest.

(v) Both Chitra and Savitri are very unhappy and sad at the end of the year.

(vi) In both the works, the heroines pray to God (Madana and Vasanta in Chitra and Yama in Savitri) and practically acquire their help.

(vii) In both the works, Time is an important factor *i.e.*, Chitra enjoys an year's union with Arjuna and Savitri is destined to lead a happy married life for an year only.

(viii) Both the works deal with a grand subject that is philosophical in nature.

(ix) In both the works, we find 'woman in action.'

(x) Both the texts conclude that love is the main source of life, it leads to self-knowledge and immortality.

The points of Contrast are as follows:

(i) There is a difference in ideology of the two heroines. Chitra longs only for happiness, which is temporary while Savitri longs for eternal happiness and wholeness, completeness and perfect-permanent union.

(ii) Chitra is a plain and an unattractive princess in man's attire whereas Savitri is a radiant, bright, calm, dignified and beautiful princess.

(iii) In *Chitra*, Chitra finds Arjuna and is enamoured by him. In order to marry him she requests the god of Love and the god of Spring to grant her only a day's perfect beauty. She marries him in complete knowledge about the impermanence of her relationship with Arjuna whereas in *Savitri*, Savitri searches out Satyavan on her own without making any request to any god. She marries him in complete knowledge about the short span of Satyavan's life.

(iv) Chitra accepts her fate whereas Savitri changes her fate with the assistance of her strong will.

(v) Both are brought up in different environments. Chitravahana brings Chitra up as a son and therefore she does not know anything about feminine delicacy and grace whereas Savitri has grown up in the lap of nature. She is wiser and maturer than Chitra.

(vi) In the case of Chitra there is no direct divine working hand whereas a divine hand works directly in the case of Savitri.

(vii) Chitra is in a haste to win the heart of Arjuna whereas Savitri takes her time and does not practice any falsehood anywhere or at anytime to win Satyavan.

(viii) Chitra wins the love of Arjuna temporarily from the gods whereas Savitri wins the love and life of Satyavan permanently from Yama.

(ix) The theme of *Chitra* is the evolution of human love while the theme of *Savitri* is the evolution of human soul.

(x) Chitra fights against Illusion whereas Savitri fights against Ignorance.

(xi) In *Chitra*, the chief characters are represented thus:

(a) Chitra: Human Desire for Love

(b) Arjuna: Seeker of Love

(c) Madana: god of Love

(d) Vasanta: god of Spring

In *Savitri* the chief characters are represented thus:

(a) Savitri: Divine Grace-Light

(b) Satyavan: Divine Truth

(c) Ashwapathy: Lord of life-energy

(d) Dyumathsena: Divine Mind

(e) Yama: Darkness of Ignorance

(xii) In *Chitra* at the end both Chitra and Arjuna part whereas in *Savitri* at the end both Savitri and Satyavan get united.

REFERENCES

1. Maharshi Veda Vyas, *Shri Mahabharata*, trans. Pandit Ramnarayan Dutt Shastry Pandeya (Gorakhpur: Geeta Press, Samvat 2045), Adhyaya: 214, Sloka: 15, 614.

2. Rabindranath Tagore, *Chitra* (Delhi: Macmillan India: 1995), 9.
3. *Ibid.*, 32.
4. *Ibid.*, 32-33.
5. *Ibid.*, 59.
6. *Ibid.*, 66.
7. *Ibid.*, 67.
8. *Ibid.*, 28.
9. *Ibid.*, 60.
10. *Ibid.*, 67.
11. *Ibid.*, 60.
12. *Ibid.*, 60.
13. K.R.S. Iyengar, *Indian Writing in English.* (Bangalore: Macmillan: 1985), 138.
14. Rabindranath Tagore, *op. cit*, 9.
15. *Ibid.*, 19.
16. *Ibid.*, 19.
17. *Ibid.*, 19.
18. *Ibid.*, 58.
19. *Ibid.*, 66.
20. *Ibid.*, 8.
21. *Ibid.*, 8-9.
22. *Ibid.*, 9.
23. *Ibid.*, 9.
24. *Ibid.*, 10.
25. Maharshi Veda Vyas, *op. cit.*, Adhyaya: 293, Sloka: 24, 1773.
26. *Ibid.*, Adhyaya: 299, Sloka: 14, 1797.
27. Sri Aurobindo, *Savitri: A Legend and a Symbol* (Pondicherry: Sri Aurobindo Ashram: 1988), Canto II, 17.
28. *Ibid.*, 17.
29. *Ibid.*, 346.
30. *Ibid.*, 410.
31. *Ibid.*, Canto I, 418.
32. *Ibid.*, 432.
33. *Ibid.*, Canto II, 461.
34. *Ibid.*, Canto III, 564.
35. *Ibid.*, Book IX, Canto I, 575.
36. *Ibid.*, Canto II, 590.
37. *Ibid.*, Canto II, 594.
38. *Ibid.*, Book X, Canto III, 633.

39. *Ibid.*, Canto III, 635.
40. *Ibid.*, 635-636.
41. *Ibid.*, Book V, Canto II, 397.
42. *Ibid*, Book VI, Canto I, 432.
43. *Ibid.*, 435.
44. *Ibid.*, Book IX, Canto II, 594.
45. *Ibid.*, Book X, Canto II, 612.
46. *Ibid.*, Canto III, 633.
47. *Ibid.*, Book XII, 724.
48. Thomas Kempis, *The Imitation of Christ*, 3.5, tr. Leo Sherley, 1952.
49. Sri Aurobindo, *op. cit.*, Book VI, Canto I, 418.
50. *Ibid.*, 435.
51. *Ibid.*, Book X, Canto IV, 648.
52. *Ibid.*, 649.
53. *Ibid.*, Book I, Canto II, 17.
54. K.R.S. Iyengar, *op. cit.*, 192.
55. Sri Aurobindo, *op. cit.*, Book I, Canto II, 17.
56. K.R.S. Iyengar, *op. cit.*, 197.

3

Tagore's *Chitra* and Aurobindo's *Savitri*: A Study in Form

Dramatic literature occupies a significant place in the domain of literary output. We realise the truth of Bharata's saying that drama arose out of the desires of the gods who prayed to Brahman in these terms, 'we want an object of diversion which must be audible as well as visible.' The prophecy regarding drama by the creator receives confirmation from this fact as well. In appeasing the angry demons Brahman stated that drama was not a monopoly of the gods alone, that all the ideas could be presented through it, and that everyone, whether in sorrow, weariness or bereavement or even a sage who has transcended such mortal afflictions would find solace and rest in the drama.

The unique and all influencing character of drama did not escape the notice of the Indian mind and we have evidence of the great regard it enjoyed as an art form. Drama claims its origin in the oldest book of the Indo-Aryans, the *Vedas*. Bharata says, 'Brahman took the Recitative from the Rig-Veda, the song from the Sama, the histrionic representation from the Yajus and the sentiments from the Atharvan.' All the four sacred Vedas were churned so to say, by Brahman to create this new art form. The Indian mind has always been religious without being dogmatic, and so Aesthetics and Poetics had no quarrel with Ethics and Philosophy in ancient India. Drama, like the other arts accepted its relationship to, and its duty towards religion and morality. It aimed at removing evil and vindicating truth, goodness and beauty. And in this task it was more effective than the other art forms in so far as it was the only audio-visual art (*Drashyam shravyam cha*) and its representation of life, therefore the more immediate and persuasive.[1]

3. THE EVOLUTION OF DRAMA

The word *drama* means, *to do* and thus drama is usually associated with the idea of action. Most often, drama is thought of as a story about events in the lives of characters. As the adjective *dramatic* indicates, the ideas of conflict, tension, contrast, and emotion are usually associated with drama. Theatre as an elitist art form is most simply defined by its designed audience, and a limited group with specialized tastes. This form ranges from the court performances of the Renaissance to modern unconventional theatre. Costume, make-up, scenery, props, lighting, music, and special effects may enhance a performance.[2]

The *New Standard Encyclopedia* defines the term 'drama' as:

> a literary composition written in dialogue to be spoken by actors. Of all the art forms, drama is one of the most personal and direct in its communication. It has an almost universal appeal and has developed in all areas and sections of the world [...]. Actors speak words written by the dramatist. The director determines to a large degree the manner of presentation. The stage designer adds his contribution in the scenery and settings. Dancers and musicians may add their arts. And, in stage drama, the response of the audience to the play's action, conflict, or theme is an essential part, affecting the way in which actors perform their roles.
>
> Aristotle called drama the imitation of nature and Shakespeare said it was a mirror held up to nature. This does not mean that drama is realistic in the way a photograph is realistic, but, rather, that it conveys genuine human emotions. Drama has always served to reflect history, and it has been a powerful force in moulding public opinion.
>
> The two classical forms of drama—those developed by the ancient Greeks—are comedy and tragedy. Many variants have been produced, including tragicomedy, melodrama, musical comedy, slapstick farce, the musical

play and other types that cannot be fitted into the strict limits of Classical comedy and tragedy. One type, the *closet drama*, is written to be read but not to be acted.[3]

Although the origins of Western Theater are unknown, most theories point to a ritual origin in ancient and prehistoric rites and religious practices, because virtually all ritual contains theatrical elements. Different schools of thought attribute origins variously to ancient fertility rites, harvest festivals, shamanism, and similar sources. The earliest period in Western theatrical history is called classical, because it encompasses the drama and theater of the classical civilizations of ancient Greece and Rome, and plays were written in Greek or Latin—the classical languages.

The first evidence of dramatic literature dates from Greece in the 6th century BC, and the first extant piece of critical writing on the origin of theater is Aristotle's *Poetics* (c. 330 BC). Aristotle claimed that Greek tragedy developed from dithyrambs—choral hymns in honour of the god Dionysus—which not only praised the god but often told a story.

According to legend, Thespis, a choral leader of the 6th century BC, created drama when he assumed the part of the leading character in a dithyrambic story. He spoke and the chorus responded. From this it was but a small step to the addition of other actors and characters, and thus, according to Aristotle, drama evolved as an independent form of literature.[4]

Greek drama flourished in the 5th century BC. Aeschylus, Sophocles, and Euripides attempted the form of tragedy. Their plays are highly formal, they are written in verse and consist of scenes (episodes) among characters (never more than three speaking characters in a scene) alternating with choral songs (odes). The stories are mostly drawn from myth or ancient history, although the focus is not on a simple retelling of a story (with which the poets often took liberties), but on a consideration of humanity's place in the world and the consequences of individual actions. Generally, little action occurred on stage and most events and information were related through dialogue and choral songs.

It is believed that comedy developed in the mid-5th century BC. The oldest extant comedies are by Aristophanes. They have a highly formal structure to be derived from ancient fertility rites. The humor consists of a mixture of satirical attacks on contemporary public figures. Domestic comedy—called Middle and New Comedy—proliferated. The plot hinges on a complication or situation revolving around love, family problems, money, or the like. The characters are stock—identifiable, simplified social types, such as a miserly father or a nagging mother-in-law. In the vast theatres, modern actors depended on subtle gestures and facial expressions and voice. The 2nd century BC was dominated by the comedies of Plautus and Terence. In the 1st century AD Seneca wrote tragedies. The content, form, and devices of Senecan tragedy—a five-act structure that included soliloquies and poetic speeches—became strongly influential in the Renaissance.

Ironically, theatre in the form of liturgical drama was reborn in Europe in the Roman Catholic Church. By the 10th century the various Church services provided possibilities for dramatic presentation. Then came the mystery, or miracle plays. Afterwards folk plays, secular farces, and pastoral dramas emerged, which influenced the evolution of the morality play in the 15th century. By the mid-16th century, a new, dynamic secular drama developed in its place.

The Renaissance began at different times in different areas of Europe and was a slow process of change in ideas and values. Renaissance theatre took on a totally new form with some classical characteristics.[5] The most important concept in Renaissance art was verisimilitude—the appearance of truth. Thus, comedy and tragedy could not be combined, choruses and soliloquies were eliminated, good was rewarded, evil was punished, characters were depicted as ideal types rather than as idiosyncratic individuals, and so on. Most significant were the three Unities of time, place, and action. Based on a passage in Aristotle, theoreticians created strict rules: a play could have only a single plot, must take place within a 24-hour period, and could occur only in one locale. The rationale was that a theater audience, knowing it had been sitting in one place for a limited time, would not believe a play that spanned several days or locations—it would defy verisimilitude and order. Adherence to such rules, rather than the response of an audience, was believed to determine the quality of a play.

Nicholas Udal's *Ralph Roister Doister* (1540), the first English comedy established divisions of act and scene and use of a unified plot. *Gorboduc* (1561), by Thomas Norton and Thomas Sackville was the first English tragedy and also the first English play.[6] Commedia was at its peak from about 1550 to 1650 and influenced everything from Turkish Puppet Theatre to the plays of Shakespeare and Molière. Renaissance drama developed in England during the reign of Elizabeth I in the latter part of the 16th century. Such playwrights as Thomas Kyd and Christopher Marlowe gave birth to the epic, dynamic, unrestrained drama that culminated in the diverse and complex work of English Theatre's greatest genius, William Shakespeare.[7]

The plays used a classical act and scene structure; employed verse (although often mixed with prose); borrowed theatrical devices from Seneca, Plautus, and the commedia dell'arte; freely intermingled tragedy, comedy, and pastoral; combined several plots; covered great expanses of time and space; mixed royalty with low-life characters; incorporated music, dance, and spectacle; and showed violence, battles, and especially blood. The subjects of tragedy tended to be historical rather than mythical, and the history was often used to make a contemporary point. Subsequent English dramatists, notably Ben Jonson, adhered more strictly to neoclassical precepts.

In the restoration drama women were allowed on the English stage for the first time since the Middle Ages. The witty, sophisticated, sexually suggestive comedies of manners of the period, especially those of William Congreve, still appeal to many. The 18th-century Theatre in much of Europe was primarily an actors' theatre. Sir Richard Steele of England wrote dramas about middle and lower-class characters in which goodness invariably triumphed. These plays were known variously as domestic drama, tearful comedy, or sentimental drama.

During the 18th century the movement known as romanticism, which concentrated on the spiritual, focused on humans and human emotion rather than reason, drew their examples from a study of the real world rather than the ideal, and glorified the idea of the artist as a mad genius unfettered by rules. Romanticism thus gave rise to a vast array of dramatic literature and production that was often undisciplined and that often substituted emotional manipulation for substantial ideas.

Then there was the development of melodrama, the most pervasive dramatic genre of the 19th century. The word *melodrama* has two meanings: a mixing of tragedy and comedy (mixed drama) and drama accompanied by music. Melodramas are usually in three acts instead of the classical five; plots revolve around the conflict between a virtuous protagonist and an evil villain. The plots include many reversals of fate. They deal with characters, strong emotional values, spectacle, and moral tone.[8]

Then came the Plays of Ideas of Bernard Shaw and Poetic plays by T.S. Eliot. Modern dramatists adopted different techniques. There is a substantial tradition of major dramatists from Ibsen, Chekhov and Shaw through to Beckett, Pinter, Stoppard and Churchill. They break the conventional attitude and beliefs and give quite a different treatment to their subjects.[9]

Indian authors, on the other hand, have been much inspired by Sanskrit drama and generally the root of their inspiration is our mythology and Upanishads. They have borrowed their subjects from the *Ramayana* and the *Mahabharata*, therefore the focus has been limited only to Sanskrit drama. The history of the Indian drama is quite independent of Western influence and it throws much light on Hindu social customs during the five or six centuries preceding the Muhammadan conquest. The earliest forms of dramatic literature in India are represented by those hymns of the *Rig-Veda.*

The words, for actor (*Nata*) and play (*Nataka*) are derived from the verb *Nat,* the Prakrit or vernacular form of the Sanskrit *nr,* 'to dance.' The name is familiar to English ears in the form of *natch,* the Indian dancing of the present day. It probably represents the beginnings of the Indian drama.[10] It must at first have consisted only of rude pantomime, in which mute mimicking gestures of hands and face accompanied the dancing movements of the body. Songs, doubtless also early formed an ingredient in such performances. The addition of dialogue was the last step in the development which was thus much the same in India and in Greece. This primitive stage is represented by the Bengal *yatras* and the *Gitagovinda.* These form the transition to the fully developed Sanskrit play in which lyrics and dialogue are blended. The earliest references to the acted drama are to be found in the *Mahabhasya* which mentions representations of the *Kansavadha,* the 'slaying of Kansa' and the *Valibandha* or 'Binding of Vali' episodes in the history of Krishna. The Indian tradition describes Bharata as having represented before the gods the *Swayamvara* of Lakshmi.[11]

From all this it seems likely that the Indian drama was developed in connection with the cult of *Vishnu-Krishna* and that the earliest acted representations were therefore, like the mysteries of the Christian Middle Ages, a kind of religious play in which scenes from the legend of the gods were enacted mainly with the aid of song and dance, supplemented with prose dialogue improvised by the performers.[12]

The drama has had a rich and varied development in India as is shown not only by the numerous plays that have been preserved, but by the native treatises on poetics, which contain elaborate rules for the construction and style of plays. Indian Sanskrit drama flourished in the 4th and 5th centuries. The dramas are primarily structured around nine *rasas,* or moods, rather than characters, because the plays are concerned primarily with spiritual matters. They use stories, however, drawn from the great Indian epics, the *Mahabharata* and the *Ramayana.* The stages were elaborately decorated, but no representational scenery was used. Movements of every part of the body, vocal delivery, and song were all strictly codified. Puppet, folk, and dance drama, especially the *kathakali,* have also been popular at various times in Indian history.[13]

Love is the subject of most Indian dramas. While the Indian drama shows some affinities with Greek comedy, it affords more striking points of resemblance to the productions of the Elizabethan playwrights and in particular of Shakespeare. The aim of the Indian dramatists is not to portray types of character, but individual persons; nor do they observe the rule of unity of time or place. They introduce romantic and fabulous elements; they mix prose with verse; they blend the comic with the serious and introduce puns and comic distortions of words. The character of the *vidushaka,* too, is a close parallel to the fool in Shakespeare. Common to both are also several contrivances such as the writing of letters, the introduction of a play within a play, the restoration of the dead to life and the use of intoxication on the stage as a humourous device. The stage scenery and decorations were of the bare minimum, much being left to the imagination of the spectator as in the Shakespearean drama.

The best productions of the Indian drama are nearly a dozen in number and date from a period embracing something like four hundred years, from about the beginning of the fifth to the end of the eighth century AD. These plays are the compositions of the great dramatists like Kalidasa and Bhavabhuti or have come down under the names of the royal patrons as Shudraka and Shriharsha. The richness of creative fancy which Kalidasa displays in *Shakuntalam, Vikramurvashiyam* and *Malavikagnimitram* and his skill in the expression of tender feeling, assign him a high place among the dramatists of the world. Here the characters are surrounded by nature with which they are in constant communion.[14]

Generally, in the Sanskrit dramatic tradition the plot is taken from mythology or history and the characters are heroic or divine; it is written in an elaborate style and is full of noble sentiments. Rabindranath Tagore bears affinity with this tradition as he himself was profoundly influenced by Indian mythology. He has taken his plot of the play *Chitra* from the *Aadi-Parva* of the *Mahabharata.* The play includes the chief characteristics of plot, character, dialogue, brevity of treatment, soliloquy, conflict, theme, costume, makeup, scenery and music. Tagore's *Chitrangada* (Bengali version) was written in 1891 and published in 1892, while its English version titled as *Chitra* was written in 1913. Tagore seems much closer to the grandly serious spirit of the other English romantics in *Chitra.* He believes in the goodness of man in terms of human relationships and preaches that true growth implied transcendence from the physical to the spiritual.

3.1. *Chitra* as a Play

Chitra was performed in India without scenery and the audience surrounded the actors. All the other necessary components for writing and producing the drama, such as playwriting, acting, costume and scenic design were attended to by Tagore. *Chitra* is based on the *Chitrangada-Arjuna* episode in the *Mahabharata*. Tagore filled this skeleton with flesh and blood of an enchanting romance, full of deep psychological insight into the relationship of man and woman. It is a dramatic sermon on the theme of true love. Arjuna, the Pandava prince spurns the princess Chitra, the daughter of the King of Manipur. Later when transformed into a beautiful damsel by a boon from the god of Love and god of Spring, she approaches Arjuna again. He is infatuated. But Chitra conquers her unease by boldly revealing the truth about her. The false woman redeems herself as the true mother-to-be. The sensual is transcended in the spiritual, and the union is consecrated at last.

Tagore's *Chitra* has a compact and neat structure. Its principal characters tend to be symbolic. Tagore's drama is firmly rooted in the Indian ethos in its themes and characters and eminently expressive of his deepest convictions in creative terms. It is interesting to know the genesis of the play. Once after one of Tagore's early visits to Shantiniketan while he was returning to Calcutta and watching the receding landscape from the window of his railway coach, he was struck by the profusion of flowers on the wild shrubs and trees that lined both sides of the track in the month of April. "These flowers so fragrant and lovely to look at would soon wither and fall in the burning heat of the sun and in their stead the trees among which were many mango trees would bear fruit. The flowers were merely the play of spring-nature's trick to induce the fruit."[15] Musing on this the young poet said to himself: "If a sensitive woman felt that her lover was bound to her solely on account of her physical charms, which were external and short-lived, and not by any qualities of her heart and the need of her life-long companionship, she would discover in her body not an asset but a rival."[16] This idea intrigued the poet and he felt like giving it a dramatic form. At the same time an episode from the *Mahabharata* floated into his mind. The two jostled in his consciousness until several years later the present drama emerged during his sojourn in a small village in Orissa, called Pandua, where he had gone to inspect his family estates.[17]

Chitra is a play in one act and nine scenes in the English version and eleven scenes in the Bengali version. The eleven scenes in the original Bengali version have been reduced to nine keeping in view the interests of the English-speaking public. The scenes vary in length from one another keeping in view their plausibility and requirement in the development of the story. *Chitra* has been performed in India without scenery—the actors being surrounded by the audience.[18]

The forthcoming paragraphs consider *Chitra* as a drama in terms of (i) Plot Construction (ii) Character (iii) Dialogue (iv) Conflict (v) Theme (vi) Supernatural Device (vii) Soliloquy (viii) Intensity of emotion and Lyrical quality in terms of Diction.

(i) Plot Construction

Chitra is a play in one act and nine scenes. Freytag pointed out that the plot of a play may be symbolized as a "pyramidal structure," its diagram consists of the exposition, the initial incident, its development, the conflict, the resolution and the catastrophe.[19] *Chitra* also consists of the exposition, the initial incident, its development, crisis, falling action and catastrophe. In the first scene, there is the rebuff of Chitra by Arjuna. Chitra tells Madana (god of Love) and Vasanta (god of Youth and Beauty) how, on seeing Arjuna, she had broken her bow and cast away her arrows, changed her boy's attire to a woman's, and approached him—only to be rejected, because of his vow of celibacy. While she knows there is a long hard way of winning him, she contemplates to take recourse to an easy way by asking for the gift of physical beauty from the gods. She then acquires it for the span of a whole year.

According to William Henry Hudson, "The plot" must have "a beginning, middle and an end."[20] In *Chitra*, the exposition which should be clear, brief, dramatic and of absolute naturalness and spontaneity, consists at first the rejection of Chitra's suit by Arjuna; her sense of inferiority due to the lack of feminine graces and charms, and her seeking the help of Madana and Vasanta. The machinery of the gods constitutes an integral part of the plot of action. It is not merely a decorative appendage. The gods granted her prayer of being endowed with beauty and extraordinary charms for a year. The playwright thus prepares a background of passion, love, romance and beauty in the very beginning against which the action here would develop. Moreover, insight into Chitra and Arjuna's character is also given here. Chitra, inspite of being attired as a warrior, with her sinews hardened is a woman after all. Arjuna who is handsome, tall and masculine turns himself away from her, for he does not find in her anything, which can entice him to her. He had taken a vow of celibacy for twelve years, which he could not violate. The charms of her body were not such as to lead him away from his resolution. The exposition of the action of *Chitra* is thus made in this scene.

In the second scene, there is the spurning of Arjuna by Chitra. When Arjuna, unmindful of his vows, seeks the new Chitra in the temple, she is more saddened than elated. And consequently she rejects Arjuna.

The story develops with Arjuna's sudden acceptance of Chitra later on, due to Chitra having been endowed with beauty and grace for a year by the gods of Love and Spring. Their amours and blissful spending of the time in the forest in a romantic setting is depicted in this scene. The triumph of the body over the soul is revealed here. Arjuna falls a prey to the appearance of perfect beauty. The Other Chitra is falsehood, an illusion, a deceit of a god. Chitra admits this to Arjuna and reveals to him obliquely her true identity. But to Arjuna everything seems to be a dream; he forgets his vow of celibacy and perceives the appearance of beauty which is now before him. She makes him a captive of her love and beauty and he desires to drink deep into the joys of her beauty and charms.

The action in the story develops due to the help of the gods.

In the third scene, one sees the physical union of Chitra and Arjuna. Then Chitra tells Madana and Vasanta that during the previous night Arjuna had come and made love to her. Yet she is full of remorse because Arjuna had not loved her but only her borrowed beauty. Her body has thus become her own enemy.

Chitra and Arjuna's union does not give Chitra a sense of satisfaction, but on the contrary it brings out the dormant anguish of her soul. Her physical beauty is a temporary one. As such it would slip away from her and she would be left to sit and weep day and night when she would be put to shame at her naked poverty. The body triumphs, but its triumph is only momentary, for it would soon fade away into nothingness. With the close of the flowering season the triumph of fruitage would follow, when the heat—cloyed bloom of the body would droop and the abiding fruitful truth would be accepted. Earthly bliss brings in its train satiety in the consummation, which the union of the two bodies enjoys. Behind this is concealed a cry of agony. This has been described in a subtle manner, which speaks of the great artistic sensibility of the poet. The two gods appear for the second time in the scene. It is through Chitra's dialogue with them that the action of the drama is further unfolded and the symbolic meaning of the play is revealed that, Man is not content with the earthly bliss (which is temporal) and he essentially longs for a bliss, which is of a higher type (which is permanent). The entire atmosphere in the scene is romantic and passionate. The language used is also romantic and poetic. There is thus perfect fusion between the theme and the language.

In the fourth scene, the decline of Arjuna's passion is described. As the days pass, there is a sharp decline in Arjuna's zeal. Now, he dreams of home. He wonders when Chitra says that such ephemeral love is not meant for familial happiness. It is difficult to say whether it is Chitra that is giving Arjuna eyes to see that mundane unfolding truth, or whether she is too self conscious, too suspicious of the consequence of their love. When she invites him again to partake of love's excess, he calls her attention to the prayer-bells from the distant temple. To Arjuna love is more than a mere reverie of the senses.

The scene shows that Arjuna is gradually awakening into his real self from the world of shadows and dreams because dreams cannot enwrap a man forever; they are to vanish and their place is to be taken by the realities of life. Chitra's remark is significant as it has a prominent bearing on the meaning of the play. Physical enjoyments beget satiety after indulgence in it for sometime. It is not abiding and one feels like turning away from it after it has been drunk to the lees.

The fifth scene is an interlude. The fervour of Vasanta (Youth and Beauty) cannot keep pace with the demands of Madana (Love). There is the inevitable awakening of spring, as it draws to a close.

Madana and Vasanta appear for the third time in this scene. They carry the action further by a comment that the earthly bliss of Chitra and Arjuna, having reached the highest point, is almost at its end. The language here is poetic, romantic, sensuous and full of passion.

In the sixth scene, further decline of Arjuna's obsession is depicted. Arjuna who readily switched over from asceticism to love now longs for the old days when he used to hunt with his brothers. Contemplation entangles, and he wonders about his companion, her home and parents.

The scene shows the development in Arjuna's character whose mind is now full of the thoughts of hunting and he reminisces. He thinks of a home where kind hearts wait for his return. His heart is dissatisfied and he expresses the need to hold on to something permanent. The year is not yet complete and he is tired. All this shows that indulgence in sensuous and physical pleasures leave a man dissatisfied. Chitra is wayward. She has no name and fixed destination. She has no ties with the world and when the time comes she droops silently without feeling sorry, for she has had the fullest in her life.

The seventh scene witnesses another interlude. Madana grants Chitra's wish that her beauty shall flash brightest on the last night of Spring. The playwright wants to suggest that the spirit of beauty is eternal. It never dies. It only changes shapes. Similarly the beauty of the spirit is also eternal.

In the eighth scene, the real Chitra comes to light. Arjuna hears from wandering villagers about the princess Chitra now gone on a journey. So he ponders about the real Chitra, whose arms with beauty of strength is a fright to the robbers. He throws the formidable task that they too—he and the beautiful woman by his side—should leave the unbearable thicket of love and race on their horses to the field of action. And this challenge provokes the appropriate response.

In this scene, Arjuna's mind is fully occupied with the thoughts of princess Chitra. He sees in her a goddess of victory, dispensing glad hope all around her. She is like a watchful lioness that protects her villagers with her fierce love. Arjuna is a changed man now. He accepts Chitra, the same from whom he had recoiled in the earlier part as she is in actual life, a warrior, denuded from womanly graces. The action shows progression and is gradually reaching to its climax.

The ninth scene leads us from falsehood to truth. Chitra returns to Arjuna as she had been when she first met Arjuna. Yet she is not quite the same, for she is also the prospective mother of Arjuna's son. Arjuna is satisfied, and has a sense of complete fulfilment and even Chitra has no remorse.

Thus, Chitra reveals herself to Arjuna in this scene and reminds him of her first meeting with him. She clarifies that woman is a helpmate of man and is not merely his plaything. This is what Tagore has visualized in the character of Chitra. Arjuna and Chitra fully wake to reality at the end of the play.

Chitra musters up courage and successfully persuades Arjuna to take the course which he thinks is the best and the truest. However Arjuna expresses satisfaction and a sense of fulfilment at what has happened. When finally they part towards the close of the play real love emerges from the ashes of their transient love. The denouement is just mentioned and the play ends. *Chitra* has a poetic beginning and it has an abrupt and unexpected end. The revelation of the real identity of Chitra does not make Arjuna feel sorry but makes him filled with a sense of contentment. Chitra and Arjuna realize that mere love and beauty cannot be the ultimate value of life. The playmate of the night claims her place as the helpmate of the day. The two together make up the complete wife. Thus, complete love is a fusion of both sensuous enjoyment and life's sterner duties.

There is no complexity in the plot. Various moods of Chitra and Arjuna are drawn sharply. The beauty of the play lies in its presentation and message than in the story. The play is not only a thing of beauty in itself but reveals to us what artistic possibilities lie in the Puranas, the *Ramayana* and the *Mahabharata*. If only we have in us the selective and creative genius of great poets like Kalidasa, Bhavabhuti, Aurobindo, and Tagore can we learn the message of such stories in the right spirit. One can then seek tó steep in these stories the light of one's imagination and reveal them to the world for its uplift and delight. The great peculiarity in the case of stories of India is that they are still a living force in the hearts of men, that the persons dealt within them are still our ideals who dominate and direct our lives and our thoughts; and that a new interpretation of such stories in a vivid manner will help to unify and intensify our national life and make our land full of dynamic love and achievement.[21]

(ii) Character

Characterisation is really the fundamental and lasting element in the greatness of any dramatic work.[22] Chitra has only four *dramatis personae,* for the villagers are lay figures; and of these four, two are immortals and the other two are mortals. The two gods come into view at usual intervals and are directly responsible for the physical union of Chitra and Arjuna. There is a gradual development of the character of Chitra; the gods also appear at regular intervals; there is a subtle inter-play of mood within mood and that although Chitra and Arjuna both experience the joys of sensuous love and both tire of it, their reactions to this experience are widely divergent. As the play opens, two meetings between Chitra and Arjuna take place. In the first meeting she meets him in the disguise of a man and in the second, as a beautiful woman. Chitra captivates Arjuna. Her dream is fulfilled and she grasps what may be called absolute joy, but she suddenly discovers that the dream is not as sweet as expected. She feels that she has degraded Arjuna by ensnaring him in the toils of mere physical beauty. She becomes painfully conscious that the rapturous embrace for which she hungered has been withdrawn by the disguise upon her. She herself begged it as a boon from the gods, but at that time she could not foresee what reaction the fulfilment of her dream would awaken in her own soul. Thus, the gods help in the development of the drama as well as in the growth of the two human characters. Edward Thompson states that "these divine actors are as adequately present as Shakespeare's elves in his enchanted woodland; they mingle in human affairs with friendly half-amused grace."[23]

Chitra gradually realizes that what is easily won may be even more easily lost. She is fully aware that there is the longer surer way—the way of devotion, *tapasya,* but she chooses the quicker way of borrowed beauty to make the assault on Arjuna's senses, rather than achieve conquest of the whole man. Arjuna too is likewise ready, (although he knows nothing about her except that she is physically alluring), to give up his vow and surrender to the moment. No wonder she is discontented and he also is unhappy. It is natural enough that beauty or glamour should attract in the first instance man to woman or woman to man; but this attraction has still to pass other tests before it can acquire the name and true nature of love. With man and woman the attraction, the coming together, is not the end, but only the beginning. It has to survive shared trials, shared sorrows, shared gradual failure of the bodily functions.[24] Chitra belongs to the earth and undergoes tremendous change in her encounter with harsh reality of life. She is full of self-respect and self-confidence.

As in the handling of plot, so also in characterization the first condition of dramatic art is brevity. The dramatist has to deal with motive and character within the narrowly circumscribed area of a comparatively few scenes, in which at the same time he has to be more or less concerned with the progress of his story. Tagore, within the short span of nine scenes has successfully dealt with his motive and has remarkably portrayed his characters. He clearly draws the error of Chitra and finally her realization of the truth of life.

(iii) Dialogue

The dialogues of the play express the ideas and emotions of the characters and thereby the intention of the playwright. "Dialogue becomes an essential adjunct to action or even an integral part of it. The story moving beneath the talk and being staged stage by stage, elucidated by it."[25] The dialogues in *Chitra* are radiant with the light of poetry and romance. They suggest the gradual development of the characters. The dialogue by Chitra in the last scene of the play is a fine example of how the character of Chitra has grown since the first scene. She says:

> I am Chitra. No goddess to be worshipped, not yet the object of common pity to brushed aside like a moth with indifference. If you deign to keep me by your side in the path of danger and daring, if you allow me to share the great duties of your life, then you will know my true self. If your babe whom I am nourishing in my womb, be born a son, I shall myself teach him to be a second Arjuna, and send him to you when the time comes, and then at last you will truly know me.[26]

Here, an Egoistic Chitra gives place to a devotional Chitra. Her ego has melted away. Her sacrifice marks out her maturity and understanding power. This love of Chitra is born of deep understanding. She is content and realizes that she is both a woman and a mother. Now she has a clear vision of life. Her passion has taught her the real meaning of love. Similarly Arjuna's mental growth and spiritual development is seen in the following lines:

> Why these tears my love? Why cover your face with your hands? Have I pained you, my darling? Forget what I said. I will be content with the present. Let each separate moment of beauty come to me like a bird of mystery from its unseen nest in the dark bearing a message of music. Let me for ever sit with my hope on the brink of its realization and thus end my days.[27]

This dialogue points out a gradual rise from the early immature judgement to the ripe understanding of the character (regarding love and life). Chitra and Arjuna uplift themselves from the physical level. They understand gradually that the body is only the temple of the soul, and not the God Himself. It is temporary, changeable and visible. But the principle element is the soul that is immortal, constant and abstract. They realize:

> Atma va are drashtavyaha shrotavyo mantavyo nididhyasitavyon maitrevyatmano va are darshanen shravanen matya vigyaneneda sarve viditam.[28]
>
> (Neither the body nor anything else is worthy of contemplation. It is only the soul that is worth seeing, listening, and meditating.)

Thus, the play is a play of passion, love and real love and therefore the dialogues are radiant with the light of romance and poetry.

(iv) Conflict

Conflict is the soul of a drama. It is the datum and very backbone of a dramatic story. "The dramatic action develops as a result of the conflict—some clash of opposed individuals, or passions, or interest."[29] The conflict may be external or internal. *Chitra* has both the kinds of conflict—external and internal. For instance, the external conflict is visible in the beginning of the play, when Arjuna does not pay attention to the suit of the love of Chitra on the plea that he was in exile and that the vow of celibacy forbade him to respond to the beauty and charms of a lady. It is with this external conflict that the play starts. Then Chitra in her conversation with Madana tells him to teach her his lessons; give her the power of the weak and the weapon of the unarmed hand.

There is an internal conflict too, which is always there in Chitra's mind when she entices Arjuna by the charms and graces bestowed on her by the gods. She is fully aware of the fact that the gods have granted to her this beauty for a year only and therefore she decides that after the end of the period when she would appear in her real self before Arjuna, she would then eventually repulse him. She therefore enjoys the period granted with fullness, but thinks continuously that Arjuna does not love her. It is her borrowed beauty that is loved by him. This inward conflict becomes pronounced when she ultimately decides that before the expiry of the period of one year she would tell Arjuna all the facts and thus lift the heavy burden off her mind by this act of penitence. Otherwise, her dream to clasp Arjuna shall get shattered. Therefore Chitra asks:

> Would it please your heroic soul if the playmate of the night aspired to be the helpmeet of the day, if the left arm learnt to share the burden of the proud right arm?[30]

Thus, Chitra realizes that complete love is a fusion of both physical enjoyment and life's unsympathetic obligations. It is this internal conflict which makes the play as one of the best plays of Tagore.

(v) Theme

Chitra exhibits a realization of the diviner elements of life and love; a heavenly message to the human soul as to what is the meaning of love in the truest sense of the term. In *Chitra*, Tagore discusses the evolution of human love from the physical to the spiritual. In the last scene Chitra tells Arjuna:

> The gift that I proudly bring you is the heart of a woman. Here have all pains and joys gathered, the hopes and fears and shames of a daughter of the dust; here love springs up struggling towards immortal life. Herein lies an imperfection which yet is noble and grand.[31]

Chitra makes her last sacrifice at Arjuna's feet. She brings from the garland of heaven the flowers of incomparable beauty to worship him. She is not as perfect as the flowers with which she worships him. She brings to him the gift of a heart of a woman, which is full of pains and pleasures, the hopes and fears and shames of a daughter of the dust. The imperfection, inspite of what it is, is noble and grand.

Further, the physical relationship between man and woman is the foundation of love, its composition is provided by their spiritual relationship. Love will find its fruition only when the mind and the heart of the lover and the beloved are completely united. This theme of transcendent love in *Chitra* is best explained through suggestion, which is the keynote of dramatic art. So Tagore instead of evidently telling so many things in so many words, merely suggests by way of symbols and images. In *Chitra* the central symbol is the offer of beauty to Chitra by the gods. She desires to win the love of Arjuna in a short span. However, that which is secured in a short duration also vanishes in a short duration. Chitra and Arjuna both gain and lose their attachment for each other as they had adopted the wrong mode of winning each other. But once they become conscious of their folly they begin to make amends. When at last they meet, Chitra tells Arjuna that their love is not for home. "Not for a home?"[32] asks Arjuna. And Chitra responds saying:

> No. Never talk of that. Take to your home what is abiding and strong. Leave the little wild flower where it was born; leave it beautifully to die at the day's end among all fading blossoms and decaying leaves. Do not take it to your palace hall to fling it on the stony floor which knows no pity for things that fade and are forgotten.[33]

Arjuna then exclaims, "Is our that kind of love?"[34] And Chitra confidently responds saying, "Yes."[35] She believes that if it implies the assertion of truth it should not be accompanied by any sense of regret whatsoever. And that what was meant for idle days should never outlive its destined span of life. One has to enjoy and rest satisfied till it lives or survives. Arjuna then exclaims that there is something amiss as he experiences having not obtained the real Chitra and then Chitra reveals her true identity. The fulfilment of love thus occurs in the last scene of the play when Arjuna meets the real Chitra with all her physical blemishes and exclaims in joy, "Beloved, my life is full."[36] Arjuna's reply is brief but perfect. Thus, when the time comes for the lovers to separate, they have no regrets for life has given them all it has to give. The poet does not place an exclusive value on mere love and beauty but that does not mean that they are less important because the responsibility of fatherhood and motherhood go side by side and one cannot be isolated from the other in a concept of pleasant existence. The play conveys the message of the fullness of love.

Thus, the purpose of the play is not the glorification of sexual surrender. Tagore has in reality an encyclopedic view of life and he is as much a poet of love and passion as he is a poet of God and religion. In *Chitra* he deals with the theme of human love that goes beyond its physical limitations in order to realize its full significance. The merger of man and woman is the marriage of true minds, an entire compass ranging from the sensual to the spiritual. It is not to be got simply or purchased but to be attained through *tapasya.* Youth and beauty are fleeting and death is inescapable; yet marriage achieves the wonder of 'beyonding' youth and beauty, and motherhood and fatherhood to achieve the miracle of continuity, the 'beyonding' of death itself. Before the gods deck her with captivating grace, Chitra is but a plain unselfconscious girl wearing a boy's attire. When the obtained grace has been shed, Chitra is still beautiful because she has known love, because she is now an expected mother.

Beauty and youth, although they may be transient are yet parts of our experience. "Wisdom lies in neither looking upon the body and its beauty as ends in themselves nor in imagining that our life could be wholly separated from the physical base. Tagore rejected both the negations. The ascetic's denial of life as well as the sensualist's denial of the spirit. The blinding maddening ecstasy of the physical union is not denied in *Chitra,* but its transience is also recognized."[37]

The poet's wonderful art and his power of conveying an endless world of meaning in the narrow span of a sentence are seen in the wonderful reply of Arjuna ("Beloved, my life is full"). The message of the play is the idea so beautifully expressed in Carew's poem on *True Beauty*:

> He that loves a rosy cheek
> Or a coral lip admires
> Or from star-like love doth seek
> Fuel to maintain his fires;
> As old Time maketh these decay,
> So his flames must waste away.
> But a smooth and steadfast mind,
> Gentle thoughts and calm desires,
> Hearts with equal love combined
> Kindle never dying fires:
> Where these are not, I despise
> Lovely cheeks or lips or eyes![38]

The poet teaches us that the love that is founded on beauty of body alone is built on insecure foundations. Beauty in human face and form is glorious, fleeting and mysterious. To the man with true vision, beauty, grace and charm that raptures the lover in his beloved's face is but a dim reflection—an imperfect revelation of the wondrous vision—of the light of the soul behind the veil of the mortal flesh. The beauty of the soul is immortal, as the soul is immortal. Love built on the beauty of the soul is built on a rock and endures forever.

Tagore is a true child of his great poetic ancestors. He has recognized and expressed the true glory of love in his works. His insight into Indian ideals and conceptions of love is very well shown in the essays that he has written interpreting the genius of Kalidasa. He says:

> The poet has shown here, as in *Kumarsambhava,* that the Beauty that goes hand in hand with Moral law is eternal, that the calm, controlled and beneficent form of Love, is its best form, that Beauty is truly charming under restraint and decays quickly when it gets wild and unfettered. This ancient poet of India refuses to recognise as its own highest glory; he proclaims that goodness is the final goal of love. He teaches us that the love of man and woman is not beautiful, not lasting, not fruitful,—so long as it is self-centred, so long as it does not beget goodness, so long as it does not defuse itself in society over son and daughter, guests and neighbours [...]. But on the altar of devotion (*tapasya*) India sits alone [...]. The Beauty that he adores is lit up by grace, modesty, and goodness; in its intensity it is true to one forever; in its range it embraces the whole universe. It is fulfilled by renunciation, ratified by sorrow and rendered eternal by religion [...]. Therefore is such love higher and more wonderful than wild and unrestrained Passion.[39]

The remarks that Tagore has made in respect to Kalidasa hold true for the poet himself. Moreover Krishna Kriplani also opines that "the play is very characteristic of the author. It represents a basic and permanent attitude of his mind and philosophy—his unification of man and nature, the latter almost an active participant in the drama of life and his concern with the perennial question, what is beauty; what is love; what is the true and enduring basis of man-woman relationship?"[40]

(vi) Supernatural Device

The supernatural devices in the form of the gods are employed as an indispensable part of the plot. The two gods—Madana—the god of Love and Vasanta—the god of Spring are introduced in three scenes out of the total nine. They are not artistic pieces only, but have a distinctly important role, which is necessary for the development of action in the play. They grant Chitra a blessing of beauty for the span of a year with the help of which she captivates Arjuna. Vasanta says in the first scene:

> Not for the short span of a day, but for one whole year the charm of spring blossoms shall nestle round thy limbs.[41]

Arjuna then meets this beauty seated by a lake looking at the image of her newborn heavenly loveliness. Similarly when Chitra asks Madana to grant her the prayer that her derived beauty should flame at its brightest on the last night, he responds by saying:

> Thou shalt have thy wish.[42]

Thus, the lovers Chitra and Arjuna could meet and understand the transient nature of physical love, which is ephemeral and fleeting, because of the two gods. Chitra then tells Arjuna the story of her innate love and her reclaimed radiance and offers her heart at his feet. Chitra's purity, tenderness, nobility, ability, dedication, dignity and beauty of her soul then charm Arjuna.

Prof. Tolman points out that "only those characteristics of the hero should be made prominent which really influence the course of the action and that these characteristics should be unmistakable."[43] In *Chitra*, Tagore has made only those characteristics prominent which affect the course of the action in the real sense of the term. That is her passionate longing for Arjuna is ultimately transformed into a deeper and real love for Arjuna. She is able to do so because of the two gods. Madana and Vasanta constitute not only a significant but also an integral part of the play. They are not merely means of adornment but rather are instrumental in making Chitra experience the meaning of real love.

(vii) Soliloquy

Soliloquy is the dramatist's means of taking us down into the hidden labyrinths of a person's nature, and of revealing those springs of conduct which ordinary dialogue provides him with no adequate opportunity to disclose.[44]

Tagore has used the device of soliloquy in *Chitra* and thereby has turned it into an appealing and effective play. The soliloquies reveal the minds of his characters. Arjuna speaks two soliloquies, while Chitra has only one in the entire play. In the second scene Arjuna speaks:

> Was I dreaming or was what I saw by the lake truly there? Sitting on the mossy turf, I mused over bygone years in the sloping shadows of the evening, when slowly there came out from the folding darkness of foliage an apparition of beauty in the perfect form of a woman, and stood on a white slab of stone at the water's brink [...]. To me the supreme fulfilment of desire seemed to have been revealed in a flash and then to have to vanished [...].[45]

This indicates the inner recesses of the heart of Arjuna. Chitra in man's attire cannot attract him but her newly born heavenly loveliness bewitches him and breaks his vow of celibacy. He, at once, falls in love with the Other Chitra. In the third scene, Chitra speaks:

> No, impossible. To face that fervent gaze that almost grasps you like clutching hands of the hungry spirit within; to feel his heart struggling to break its bounds urging its passionate cry through the entire body—and then to send him away like a beggar—no, impossible [...].[46]

This is the yearning cry of Chitra that prepares her to move a step further in the process of realizing her true potential. Similarly, in the sixth scene Arjuna speaks:

> I woke in the morning and found that my dreams had distilled a gem. I have no casket to enclose it, no king's crown whereon to fix it, no chain from which to hang it, and yet have not the heart to throw it away. My Kshatriya's right arm, idly occupied in holding it, forgets its duties.[47]

Thus begins Arjuna's yearning to get nearer to Chitra's soul. He also longs to go back and resume his royal duties of being helpful to his subjects though his love for the Other Chitra is still the dominant passion of his heart. But gradually, he rises to a more elevated level of love. In essence, the soliloquies reveal the innermost ideas of the characters. Further, it is well known that soliloquies are an integral part of the form of drama and hence (as exemplified by these illustrations) its inclusion in *Chitra* as an effective dramatic medium justifies the play as being categorized as a play with lyrical qualities.

(viii) Intensity of Emotion and Lyrical Quality

Chitra is full of passion and romance. Chitra displays inflamed and passionate emotion in her addresses to the gods—Madana and Vasanta and Arjuna. For instance in the third scene she says:

> Ah, god of love, what fearful flame is this with which thou hast enveloped me! I burn, and I burn whatever I touch![48]

And again she adds:

> Heaven and earth, time and space, pleasure and pain, death and life merge together in an unbearable ecstasy [...][49]

It is observed that here 'Passion' initiates the process of becoming of a person. Normally speaking, most of us are marking time throughout our lives. Most of our beings are at rest. In passion, the body and the spirit seek expression outside of self. 'Passion' is all that is other from 'self.' Sex is only interesting when it releases passion. The more extreme and the more expressed that passion is, the more unbearable does life seem without it. It reminds us that if passion dies or is denied, we are partly dead and that soon, come what may, we will be wholly so. The play does demonstrate the working of passions and its consequences. That Chitra and Arjuna realize the transcient nature of physical passion and move up to higher levels amply proves the importance of passion in human life for it provides the basis for individual growth and development.

Chitra includes spontaneity of expression, remarkable beauty, sweetness of diction, poetic touch, melody rhythm of music and imaginative faculty. For instance in the first scene Vasanta says to Chitra:

> Not for the short span of a day, but for one whole year the charm of spring blossoms shall nestle round thy limbs.[50]

Or when Chitra tells Arjuna:

> Whom do you seek in these dark eyes, in these milk-white arms, if you are ready to pay for her the price of your probity? [...] Alas, that this frail disguise, the body, should make one blind to the light of the deathless spirit.[51]

Or in the fifth scene when Madana says to Vasanta:

> Pleasure-winged days fly fast, and the year, almost at its end, swoons in rapturous bliss.[52]

We find in these illustrations almost all the lyrical qualities that have been stated above. "*Chitra* is the quintessence of romance. The speeches burn with passion, and light up the way from truth to illusion and gain the arduous climb from illusion to truth."[53] It is a wonderful piece of work as beautiful in its thought as in its expression. It begins as a play of passionate love and rises to the height of pure love. It is a love-idyll. E.J. Thompson opines that the English version titled as *Chitra* "has a swiftness of action which the Bengali text lacks."[54]

The third scene abounds in beautiful passages suggestive of a romantic atmosphere and containing expressions of passionate love. Tagore's description is marked by an unusual kind of restraint. The description of the physical features of Chitra is rather strictly limited and his description more or less relates to the natural environment. There cannot be better and a more dignified manner of expressing the supreme fulfilment of love.

Thus, *Chitra* is not a lyrical drama, as it is not written in verse. It can be called a drama with lyrical quality, as sometimes the expressions are musical and passionate. Whereas *Chitrangada*, the original Bengali text is a lyrical drama written in blank verse. In other words, *Chitra* is a "succinct Tagorean version of Kalidasa's *Shakuntala.*"[55] The play is doubtlessly one of the most fascinating and the most satisfying of Tagore's plays.

The *Mahabharata* is also the source of Aurobindo's *Savitri.* Aurobindo has taken *the Savitri-Satyavan episode* from the *Mahabharata* and has treated it in his own style in order to fulfil his aim (which he has discussed in his *The Life Divine*)—the issue between intimidating Death and the hope of New Life—an extraordinary future possibility. Aurobindo has designed this philosophy on a grand epic scale and therefore it is necessary to take into consideration the definition, classification and the outstanding features of the epic form.

3.2. The Evolution of the Epic

According to M.H. Abrams:

> Epic is a long narrative poem on a serious subject, told in a formal and elevated style, and centred on a heroic or quasi-divine figure on whose actions depends the fate of a tribe, a nation, or the human race.[56]

In other words, the epic is a long narrative poem, majestic both in theme and style. Generally, epics deal with legendary or historical events of national or universal significance, involving action of broad sweep and grandeur. Most epics deal with the exploits of a single individual and it is upon his actions that the fate of an entire tribe or community or nation depends. This element gives unity to the composition. Typically, an epic involves the introduction of supernatural forces that shape the action, conflict in the form of battles or other physical combat, and certain stylistic conventions—an invocation to the Muse, a formal statement of the theme, long lists of the protagonists involved, and set speeches couched in elevated language. Commonplace details of everyday life may appear, but they serve as background for the story, and are described in the same lofty style as the rest of the poem.

The *New Standard Encyclopedia* defines the term epic as a long narrative poem relating the deeds of a traditional or historical hero or heroes. Aristotle, using Homer's works as a model set the rules for epic poetry more than two thousand years ago. He said the characters must be of a lofty type and consistently presented in one great and complex action. A stately but simple style and fullness of detail were essential.

The folk, or national, epics grew from the earliest experience of nature and life by imaginative people. Mythology (their interpretation of nature) and legend (their idealization of history) were the elements of the epic. The real poet was the people. Even the *Iliad* and the *Odyssey*, although credited to Homer, were largely the work of the Greek people. Homer, whether an individual poet or the name of a group of poets, gave the stories their final form.

The *Odyssey* probably began as the story of a struggle between people who lived on opposite coasts of the Aegean Sea. The story was passed from man to man, from generation to generation. Gradually older stories, legends, and myths were brought into the original tale. The gods were included. New incidents were added. The chief actors were represented more dramatically. Poet, priest, and reciter, as they passed the expanding story on, added touches of imagination or more vivid characterization. Gradually, it became a summing up of Greek thought about God, nature, and man. Finally, it was put into its finished form by Homer or a group of poets. The Hindu or Sanskrit epics are even older than the Greek and were produced in a similar way.

The literary, or art epic is the work of an individual, but attempts to imitate the style of the folk epic. That is, it is a heroic narrative of elevated and finished style. It is built up about some great theme or thought that is of universal, or at least of national, importance. The central theme of Virgil's *Aeneid* is the adventures of Aeneas and his men after the Trojan War; of Milton's *Paradise Lost*, the fall of man.

The name epic has been applied to many poems that do not follow Aristotle's rule. Like "Saga," "epic" has lost much of its original meaning. Any fairly elaborate motion picture is apt to be labeled an "epic."[57]

Thus, Epic verse may be classified as:

1. The epic of growth, or popular/folk epic or primary epic:

The epics of growth, or the popular/folk epics or the primary epics are believed to have developed from the orally transmitted folk poetry by tribal bards or other authors and were eventually written down by anonymous poets. They are not the works of a single man. The primary epics deal with heroic deeds in order that such deeds may not be forgotten. In fact, they are as C.S. Lewis says, "oral poetry" in the sense that they reach their audience through the medium of recitation. The well-known examples of the folk epic are the Anglo-Saxon *Beowulf*, the German *Nibelungenlied*, and the Indian epics (*Mahakavyas*), the *Mahabharata* and the *Ramayana*. The story material appearing in folk epics is usually based on legends or events that occurred a long time before the epic itself appeared. The characters and episodes that appear in many folk epics had, in several cases, been treated in folk songs before the epic was composed. Examples of this consolidation of material are the French folk epics known as *Chansons de geste*, or songs of heroic deeds, composed from the end of the 10th to the middle or end of the 11th century, the most famous of which is the *Chanson de Roland*.[58]

2. The epic of art, or the literary epic or the secondary epic:

On the other hand, the epics of art, or the literary epics or the secondary epics are works of art deliberately planned in the epic manner, in imitation of their original prototype. They are comparatively late products. The Secondary epics are poems composed at leisure, fully revised and available for reading and re-reading. They are interesting not for their story, but for their vision and style that creates a New World of poetic reality. The well-known examples of this type of epic are, Virgil's *Aenied*, Tasso's *Jerusalem Delivered*, Spenser's *The Faerie Oueene*, Milton's *Paradise Lost*, Camoens' *Lusiad*, among others. Each is the product of an individual genius.[59]

Taking into consideration both the types of the epic the most prominent characteristics of the form are as follows:

(1) The epic is divided into Books, usually twelve in number.

(2) The epic begins with a prayer to the Muse.

(3) The epic deals with a serious-grand subject. It is usually inspired from a very well-known traditional story.

(4) The epic is centred on a heroic or quasi-divine figure on whose actions depends the fate of a tribe, a nation or the human race.

(5) The great action of an epic must be told in a grand-elevated style. Stateliness and sublimity always characterizes an epic.

(6) Super-natural agents often influence the action of the epic.

(7) The epic contains a number of thrilling episodes, such as the mustering of troops, battles, duel, wanderings of the hero, and ordeals. Moreover the description of seasons, sunrise, sunset, dawn, night, weddings, forest, mountains, and rivers is also given. On account of these episodes Nature is described in detail.

(8) Inspite of various descriptions and digressions, the epic must appear as an organic whole. The epic poet must observe the principles of unity and coherence.

(9) The theme of the epic deals with sublimity. Generally it deals with a distinctly higher ideal.

(10) The canvass of an epic is vast; it embraces heaven and earth. The hero plants his feet like a Colossus, in all the regions.

(11) An epic must have a beginning, middle and an end. Sometimes the epic poet plunges in *medias res,* in the middle of things, assuming that the readers are familiar with all the incidents.

(12) The epic poets weave the romantic emotion along with other emotions.

(13) The epic is normally full of repetitions of certain select phrases, of groups, of lines and epithets and of passages.

(14) The epic generally ends with a ray of hope—on a note of optimism—for a better human life.

3.3. *Savitri* as an Epic

Aurobindo's *Savitri* combines in itself the characteristics of both the folk and the literary epics. The following are the characteristics that are observed in *Savitri*:

1. *Savitri* is written in three parts, which comprises of twelve books and forty-nine cantos, making up a total of about 24,000 lines.
2. Aurobindo does not introduce the invocation in the

beginning of the epic. But he invokes the Divine Mother (in the Third Book) to incarnate in order to remove the badge of pain and suffering from the earth. In response to his prayer, the Divine Mother replies:

> O Son of Strength who climbst creation's peaks,
> No soul is thy companion in the light; [...]
> Man is too weak to bear the Infinite's weight.
> Truth born too soon might break the imperfect earth.[60]

The opening line quietly focuses our attention on a particular hour of the night: "It was an hour before the Gods awake"[61]—the hour between midnight and dawn. Nothing extraordinary, yet compact with mighty symbolic significance.

3. The subject of the epic is also grand. It is taken from the *Mahabharata.* The legend of Savitri and Satyavan is well-known to each and every Indian. It's a story of a *pativrata* wife who saves her husband from the clutches of Death. Savitri demands:

   > Release the soul of the world called Satyavan
   > Freed from thy clutch of pain and ignorance
   > That he may stand master of life and fate,
   > Man's representative in the house of God
   > The mate of Wisdom and the spouse of Light,
   > The eternal bridegroom of the eternal bride.[62]

4. Savitri is a human figure. She is every inch a woman who grows like a princess, falls in love with Satyavan, loves and cares for him, worries like an ordinary woman on account of the prophecy made *vis-a-vis* Satyavan. In spite of all this, she is powerful and strong-willed. She is a figure that is of cosmic importance. Like Milton's Adam, Savitri represents the entire human race. She does not only save her husband but the whole of the human race. She stands for the Divine Grace—Divine Light. Her triumph over Death is certainly a superhuman deed of spiritual adventure. Aurobindo writes about her:

   > In her the superhuman cast its seed.
   > Inapt to fold its mighty wings of dream
   > Her spirit refused to hug the common soil [...]

Her being conscious of its divine founts
Asked not from mortal frailty pain's relief, [...]
A work she had to do, a word to speak;
Writing the unfinished story of her soul
In thoughts and actions graved in Nature's book.[63]

5. *Savitri* is written in a grand style. The action of *Savitri* is narrated in a ceremonial style, which is sometimes deliberately distanced from ordinary speech and proportioned to the grandeur and formality of a spiritual subject. Hence, there are Latinate diction, stylized syntax and wide-ranging allusions and symbolic interpretations. Aurobindo in the First Book writes:

   The world was a conception and a birth
   Of Spirit in Matter into living forms,
   And Nature bore the Immortal in her womb,
   That she might climb through him to eternal life.[64]

   In the Seventh Book Aurobindo alluding to the various forms of the Divine Mother says that Savitri is:

   [...] Krishna and Radha for ever entwined in bliss
   The Adorer and Adored self-lost and one.[65]

6. The action of *Savitri* involves supernatural deeds. She boldly encounters the god of Death and snatches from him the life of her husband. The god of Death is thus indirectly responsible for arousing the latent divinity of Savitri. He attempts to threaten Savitri thus:

   I am Kali black and naked in the world
   I am Maya and the universe is my cheat.[66]

7. *Savitri* describes various episodes as the journeys of Ashwapthy from *'The Kingdom of Subtle Matter,' 'The Glory and Fall of Life,' 'The Kingdom of the Little Life,' 'The Godheads of the Little Life,' 'The Kingdoms and Godheads of the Greater Life,' 'The World of Falsehood, the Mother of Evil, and the Sons of Darkness,' 'The Paradise of the Life-Gods,' 'The Kingdoms and Godheads of the Little Mind,' 'The Kingdoms and Godheads of the Greater Mind,' 'The Heavens of the Ideal,' 'The Self of Mind,' 'The World Soul,'* to *'The House of the Spirit and the New Creation;'* Savitri's birth, parentage and education

in the lap of Nature in *'The Book of Birth and Quest;'* her marriage to Satyavan and their life in the forest in '*The Book of Love*;' the death of Satyavan in '*The Book of Death*;' Savitri's encounter with Yama, the god of Death in '*The Book of the Double Twilight*,' and her ultimate victory in '*The Book of Everlasting Day*.'

8. Despite various episodes, Aurobindo observes unity and coherence in *Savitri*. Every Book and every Canto is connected to the next in terms of theme and structure. And this makes the work organic in nature.
9. The theme of *Savitri* is ennobling and sublime. It deals with spirituality. It explains the evolution and power of human love. Aurobindo in the Fifth Book writes:

   Love brought power out of eternity [...]
   Love is glory from eternity's spheres [...]
   Love dwells in us like an unopened flower [...]
   Love's adoration like a mystic seer
   Through vision looks at the invisible [...].[67]

   The poet has linked the earthly life with the Life Divine and has reconciled external realities with inner experiences. Savitri's encounter with Death is really the struggle between the forces of Knowledge and Ignorance in which Knowledge ultimately triumphs.
10. The scope of Savitri is cosmic; its action takes place on earth, in heaven and in hell. Savitri as well as Ashwapathy traverse the subtle worlds. Ashwapathy's journey through mystic worlds reminds us of Dante's journey through hell, purgatory and paradise. Ashwapathy descends to the realm of matter and sees the process of evolution as well as the perversion of human life. Ashwapathy perceives mankind aspiring to get rid of matter's weight by pigmy thought, intelligence and reason. Like Dante, Ashwapathy ascends to the heaven of the ideals and meets the Divine Mother. But unlike Dante, Ashwapathy invokes the Divine Mother to incarnate in order to remove the badge of pain and suffering from earth. To Ashwapathy's prayer the Divine Mother responds back saying:

O Strong forerunner I have heard thy cry.
One shall descend and break the iron Law [...]
A seed shall be sown in Death's trememdous hour,
A branch of heaven transplant to human soil [...].[68]

In the later Books Savitri rises to the supra-cosmic realm of Ever-lasting Day.

11. *Savitri* is a large and complete interpretation by Aurobindo. He says:

    One artistic method is to select a limited subject and even on that to say only what is indispensable; what is centrally suggestive and leave the rest for the imagination or understanding of the reader. Another method which I hold to be equally artistic or if you like, architectural is to give a large and even vast, a complete interpretation, omitting nothing that is necessary, fundamental to the completeness: that is the method I have chosen in Savitri.[69]

    The action of *Savitri* starts in *medias res,* in the middle of the things. The epic opens with the description of the particular dawn that heralds the day on which Satyavan is destined to die. Aurobindo in the first Canto of the First Book writes:

    Amid the trivial sounds, the unchanging scene,
    Her soul arose confronting Time and Fate
    Immobile in herself she gathered force.
    This was the day when Satyavan must die.[70]

    The first canto tells us about the imminent crisis in the life of the central character, Savitri. The rest of the epic depicts her growth, marriage and her encounter with Death.

12. Like *Ramayana, Savitri* is a kind of vast romance. The Fifth Book in particular is the Book of Love, which deals with Savitri's decision to get married to Satyavan. In the Sixth Book, Aurobindo describes in detail the marital bliss of Savitri and Satyavan. A number of parallels can be observed between *Ramayana* and *Savitri.* Both are poems of dharma, and both illustrate almost all forms of love and compassion. In *Savitri,* it is love that conquers Death.

13. Like Homer, Aurobindo also repeats the key ideas, phrases, epithets and situations in Savitri. He justifies these repetitions on the following grounds:

    The repetition of the same ideas, key ideas and symbols, key words and phrases, key epithets, sometimes key lines or half-lines is a constant feature. They give an atmosphere, a significant structure, a sort of psychological frame, an architecture. The object here is not to amuse or entertain but the self-expression of an inner truth, a seeing of things and ideas not familiar to the common mind [...]. He (the mystic poet) uses *avritti*, repetition, as one of the powerful means of carrying home what has been thought or seen and fixing it in the mind in an atmosphere of light and beautiful. This kind of repetition I have largely used in Savitri.[71]

    Here is an illustration from Book I, Canto I. The single revelation, a ray of divine light showing itself and soon vanishing is repeatedly described thus:

    (a) Then the divine afflatus, spent, withdrew....
    (b) Only a little the God light can stay....
    (c) A spark diety lost in Matter's crypt....
    (d) That transitory glow of magic fire
    So now dissolved in bright accustomed air....
    (e) The excess of beauty natural to God-kind
    Could not uphold its claim on time-born eyes....
    (f) Too mystic-real for space-tenancy
    Her body of glory was expunged from heaven....
    (g) The rarity and wonder lived no more.

    Here is repetition, but each time it is a different intensity of rhythm, a different note of sound, a different image; as if it were ictuses of revealing lustre continually falling one after another on the slumbering mind and rousing it to a new awareness.

14. *Savitri* is a cosmic epic. It ends at the possibility of a greater dawn· *i.e.*, the dawn of the super-mind, which will help man attain his self-perfection. Aurobindo emphasizes that one has to realize one's soul in order to achieve one's lost divinity. Savitri's confrontation with Death is essentially the struggle between Knowledge

and Ignorance and ultimately Knowledge triumphs over Ignorance. Aurobindo writes in the last book following Savitri's victory over Death and the rising of a new dawn,

> She brooded through her stillness on a thought
> Deep-guarded by her mystic folds of light,
> And in her bosom nursed a greater dawn.[72]

Though *Savitri* combines the distinguishing features of both the epics (epic of growth and epic of art), actually speaking it is a new kind of epic poetry from the viewpoints of its thematic treatment and technique. And therefore *Savitri* is commonly referred as an epic of the soul. Unlike *The Divine Comedy* and *Paradise Lost* it deals with spirituality. Sri Aurobindo states:

> The epics of the soul most inwardly seen as they will be by an intuitive poetry, are his greatest possible subject, and it is this supreme kind that we shall expect from some profound and mighty voice of the future. His indeed will be the song of the greatest flight that will reveal from the highest pinnacle and with the largest field of vision the destiny of the human spirit and presence and ways and purpose of the Divinity in man and the universe.[73]

As an epic of the soul *Savitri* stresses that the world is the manifestation of the divine and therefore it is meaningful. It also reveals that man is not just *an image of clay*; he is really a Son of God. As such his final destiny is to become God:

> A mutual debt binds man to the supreme;
> His nature we must put on as ours;
> We are the sons of God and must be even as he;
> His human portion, we must grow divine.[74]

Savitri foreknowledges that man is to emerge as superman after the descent of the Supermind in the terrestial consciousness. And therefore the action takes place in the soul of man. Ashwapathy's journey and Savitri's quest for the soul are really limitless extensions of the psyche. Savitri conquers death with the help of her spiritual powers in the subtle planes of consciousness. The vastness and comprehensiveness of the Vedas and the Upanishads can also be traced in *Savitri.* Just as the Vedas and the Upanishads reveal that the Brahman is the ultimate reality (it is He who has manifested the universe and therefore this universe is real and a veritable source of delight and the common people are unable to experience delight because they are tied to ignorance), *Savitri,* too emphasizes that the Absolute is the substratum of the universe and that if man's soul is free from Ignorance, he can experience bliss amidst sorrows and sufferings.

Thus, *Savitri* is an inspired expression of the very spirit of India. Here the centralization of interest in the character constitutes the grandeur of *Savitri.* Therefore *Savitri* is distinguished from all other epics of the world. Professor Raymond Frank Piper rightly states,

> Savitri is perhaps the most powerful artistic work in the world for expanding man's mind towards the Absolute.[75]

3.4. The Comparison between the Play *Chitra* and the Epic *Savitri*

Aristotle in his *Poetics* has discussed tragedy (drama) and epic in chapters V, XXIII, XXIV and XXVI. In his discussion of epic poetry, he has developed some of the points and goes into further detail on the important question of the nature of poetic truth. His account of the epic and drama is of special interest in this chapter because the points of comparison between the forms of *Chitra* and *Savitri* can accordingly be traced out:

1. The drama is short and is confined to a single revolution of the sun; it deals with a single action, one that is a complete whole itself, with a beginning, a middle and an end, so as to enable the work to produce its own proper pleasure with all the organic unity of a living creature. Whereas the epic is a long narrative poem, which includes many incidents.

   Chitra consists of only one act and nine scenes. It deals with a single action, which is complete and of a definite magnitude. It is a story that begins with Chitra's passionate love at first-sight for Arjuna; the middle consists of Chitra's request to the gods Madana and Vasanta for being endowed with perfect beauty for a day and her being granted that for an year; and the end deals with Chitra and Arjuna's realization and transcendence from the material/physical to the eternal/ spiritual.

On the other hand, *Savitri* is a long narrative poem in twelve books with incidents ranging from the *tapasya* of Ashwapathy; to the birth of Savitri; her marriage with Satyavan; Satyavan's death; her encounter with the god of Death; Savitri's ultimate victory over Death and Savitri and Satyavan's return to the earth.

2. The drama includes six constituent parts in it such as Plot, Character, Thought, Diction, Song and Spectacle. While the epic has only four parts with the exception of Song and Spectacle.

Chitra includes the *Chitrangada-Arjuna* plot of the *Mahabharata*: Chitra and Arjuna as mortal and Madana and Vasanta as immortal characters; the thought that complete love is a fusion of both sensuous enjoyment and life's sterner duties; the matter-of-fact diction; Song in the form of music and Spectacle in the form of audience (during its presentation). Incidently, *Chitra* has vividness of impression in reading as well in representation.

On the other hand, *Savitri* has the *Savitri-Satyavan* plot of the *Mahabharata*: Savitri and Satyavan, Ashwapathy and his wife, Dyumatsena and his wife among the mortal and Narada and the god of Death among the immortal characters; the thought that life-divine is possible on earth only when one realizes one's soul in order to achieve one's lost divinity. (This is the struggle between knowledge and ignorance and ultimately knowledge triumphs over ignorance); and the diction by way of style is grand, ceremonial, distanced from ordinary speech and proportioned to the grandeur and formality of a spiritual subject. As the epic *Savitri* is essentially a long-narrative, the elements of Song and Spectacle automatically do not form a part of its composite structure.

3. The drama deals with action (*abhinaya*) while the epic deals with narration.

   Chitra is dramatic in form and deals with the principal action of Chitra's longing to possess Arjuna at all costs. While *Savitri* is narrative in form and deals with significant incidents which take place in the life of Savitri and Satyavan.

4. The drama admits of many kinds of meter but the epic admits of only one kind of meter *i.e.* the heroic meter.

   Chitra as a play admits of dialogue in prosaic-poetry, while *Savitri* as an epic has blank verse as the medium of expression.

5. The drama includes all the secondary accessories—dialogue, song, scenery, spectacle, costume, and make-up, whereas the epic is a narrative form therefore it deals with no secondary aids.

   Chitra as a play deals with the secondary accessories of the dialogue (between Chitra, Arjuna, Madana and Vasanta); and song, spectacle, scenery, costume, and make-up during its presentation on the stage. While *Savitri* as a narrative has no secondary accessories/ aids in it.

6. The drama requires less space for the attainment of its end, which is a great advantage since the more concentrated effect is more pleasurable than one with a large admixture of time to dilute it, while there is less unity in the imitation of the epic poets as is proved by the fact that any one work of theirs supplies matter for several plays.

   Chitra as a play requires only one act and nine scenes for the communication of Tagore's message. However *Savitri*, by way of having a number of episodes in the twelve Books carries in itself a matter for so many plays. There is thus organic unity to be clearly seen in *Chitra*, which of course, does not imply that there is an absence of unity in *Savitri*. In fact, the thread of unity runs at a sublime level through the twelve books of *Savitri*.

7. Both the drama and the epic have a central character around whom the action of the entire play/epic revolves.

   Both *Chitra* and *Savitri* have Chitra and Savitri as their main characters. It is around them that the action of the play *Chitra* and the epic *Savitri* grows and develops. It is also striking that the female characters Chitra and Savitri are the main characters so much so that the works are titled after the names of the heroines and not after the names of the heroes. The object of both the play as well as the epic is to present the illustrious lives of remarkable women. They ennoble human life and advocate the value of Truth.

Thus, it does not really matter whatever the length of a text may be, because the length is not the criteria for assessing the value of a work of art. Bulk or difference in form is not the real measure of a good piece of literature. *The Critical Idiom* aptly states, "Epic is not a matter of length or size, but of weight."[76] Even the difference in form does not harm the artistic presentation of a literary work. On the contrary, it is the difference in the form (the play *Chitra* and the epic *Savitri*) which includes the real study of comparison. It is the conception of life that it presents and treats and the value and permanence of a work of art lies upon this one fact. So, *Chitra* is no less artistic a work of art. It is as condensed as *Savitri* is. *Chitra* is the articulation of *Sundaram* whereas *Savitri* is the articulation of *Shivam* and both invariably and definitely show us the exposition of *Satyam*.

REFERENCES

1. Ramkrishna Shastri, *Sanskrit Drama and Dramaturgy* (Madras: Prakash Deep Publications: 1965), 1-2.
2. *Simon and Schuster Encyclopedia* (CD).
3. *New Standard Encyclopedia* Vol. IV (DE) (Chicago: Standard Educational Corporation: 1981), D-259.
4. *Simon and Schuster Encyclopedia* (CD).
5. *Ibid.*
6. *New Standard Encyclopedia* Vol. IV (DE) (Chicago: Standard Educational Corporation: 1981), D-260.
7. *Simon and Schuster Encyclopedia* (CD).
8. *Ibid.*

9. John Peck and Martin Coyle, *Literary Terms and Criticism* (London: The Macmillian Press Limited: 1995), 104.
10. A.A .Macdonell, *A History of Sanskrit Literature* (Delhi: Munshi Ram Manoharlal Oriental Publishers and Booksellers: 1961), 349.
11. *Ibid.*, 351.
12. *Ibid.*, 357.
13. *Ibid.*, 357.
14. *Ibid.*, 357.
15. Krishna Kriplani, *Rabindranath Tagore: A Biography* (London: Macmillan Ltd.: 1980), 144.
16. *Ibid.*, 144.
17. *Ibid.*, 144.
18. Rabindranath Tagore, *Chitra* (New Delhi: Macmillan India Limited: 1995), ix.
19. William Henry Hudson, *An Introduction to the Study of Literature* (New Delhi: Kalyani Publishers: 1979), 201.
20. *Ibid.*, 205.
21. K.S. Ramaswami Sastri, *Sri Rabindranath Tagore: His Life, Personality and Genius* (Delhi: Akashdeep Publishing House: 1988), 266.
22. William Henry Hudson, *op. cit.*, 186.
23. Edward Thompson, *Rabindranath Tagore: Poet and Dramatist* (Delhi: Oxford University Press: 1989), 137-38.
24. K.R.S. Iyengar, *Indian Writing in English* (New Delhi: Sterling Publishers Private Limited: 1995), 137-138.
25. William Henry Hudson, *op. cit.*, 187.
26. Rabindranath Tagore, *Chitra* (Delhi: Macmillan India Limited: 1995), 66-67.
27. *Ibid.*, 61.
28. *Sri Upanishada.* (Gondal: Shri Bhagavadsinghji Electric and Litho Printing Press: 1938), Brihadarnayaka, 2, 4, 5, 530.
29. William Henry Hudson, *op. cit.*, 199.
30. *Chitra. op. cit.*, 60.
31. *Ibid.*, 66.
32. *Ibid.*, 32.
33. *Ibid.*, 32.
34. *Ibid.*, 32.
35. *Ibid.*, 32.
36. *Ibid.*, 67.
37. *Indian Writing in English, op. cit.*, 138.
38. Quoted in K.S.Ramaswami Sastri. *op. cit.*, 267.
39. *Indian Writing in English, op. cit.*, 136.

40. Krishna Kriplani, *Rabindranath Tagore: A Biography* (London: Macmillan Ltd.: 1980), 143.
41. *Chitra. op. cit.*, 10.
42. *Ibid.*, 49.
43. William Henry Hudson, *op. cit.*, 188-89.
44. William Henry Hudson, *op. cit.*, 195-96.
45. *Chitra. op. cit.*, 13-14.
46. *Ibid.*, 23.
47. *Ibid.*, 41.
48. *Ibid.*, 23.
49. *Ibid.*, 25.
50. *Ibid.*, 10.
51. *Ibid.*, 19.
52. *Ibid.*, 37.
53. *Indian Writing in English, op. cit.*, 136-37.
54. Edward Thompson, *op. cit.*, 118.
55. *Indian Writing in English, op. cit.*, 136.
56. M.H. Abrams, *A Glossary of Literary Terms* (Delhi: Macmillan India Limited: 1987), 49.
57. *New Standard Encyclopedia* Vol. IV (DE) (Chicago: Standard Educational Corporation: 1981), E-190.
58. *Simon and Schuster Encyclopedia* (CD).
59. *Ibid.*
60. Sri Aurobindo, *Savitri: A Legend and A symbol* (Pondicherry: Sri Aurobindo Ashram: 1988), Book III, Canto IV, 335.
61. *Ibid.*, Book I, Canto I, 1.
62. *Ibid.*, Book X, Canto IV, 666.
63. *Ibid.*, Book I, Canto II, 19.
64. *Ibid.*, Book I, Canto III, 43.
65. *Ibid.*, Book VII, Canto V, 525.
66. *Ibid.*, Book VII, Canto VI, 535.
67. *Ibid.*, Book V, Canto II, 397-98.
68. *Ibid.*, Book III, Canto IV, 346.
69. Sri Aurobindo, *Letters on Savitri* (Pondicherry: Sri Aurobindo University Centre collection, Vol. II, 792.
70. *Savitri. op. cit.*, Book I, Canto I, 09.
71. *Letters on Savitri. op. cit.*, 740.
72. *Savitri. op. cit.*, Book XII, 724.
73. Sri Aurobindo, *The Future Poetry* (Pondicherry: Sri Aurobindo Ashram: 1953), 367-77.

74. *Savitri. op. cit.*, Book I, Canto IV, 67.
75. *Indian Writing in English, op. cit.*, 206.
76. John D. Jump, (ed.) *The Critical Idiom* (London: Metheun and Co. Ltd.: 1971), 94.

4

TAGORE'S *CHITRA* AND AUROBINDO'S *SAVITRI*: A STUDY IN PHILOSOPHY

4. THE PHILOSOPHY OF TAGORE IN *CHITRA*

Tagore did not propound a philosophy that was of the usual type and he does not arrive at the concept of Reality or the Absolute through the process of logical deduction. He owes it directly to his early intuitive vision. While describing his second vision, he says:

> I felt sure that some Being who comprehended me and my world was seeking his best expression in all my experiences.[1]

The poet is thus convinced by the direct vision that beneath the changing phenomena there dwells the eternal Spirit beyond the reach of our senses. He speaks of this eternal Spirit as God, Infinite, Supreme Person, Supreme Being, Bridegroom or Lover, Friend, Father, Master, King and so on.

Regarding the nature of the ultimate reality, Tagore holds the view that it is One, He observes:

> Facts occupy endless time and space; but the truth comprehending them all has no dimension; it is One. Wherever our heart touches the One, in the small or the big, it finds the touch of the infinite.[2]

The Ultimate Reality or the Absolute for Tagore implies Peace or Harmony, Bliss and the Non-Dual.

Peace or Harmony is that serenity by means of which the entire universe (with all the planets and stars) is poised in peace and harmony and by means of which the propelling time is organized within the hold of eternity. It is called Peace because as the poet thinks, all its established laws are in harmony with one another. He feels that there is harmony between the infinite and the finite, and between nature and man. The immanence of Reality has to be realized in external nature as well as in the inmost human recesses. The concept of Harmony provides relief from passivity, despair and pessimism. In place of chaos, confusion, disorderliness or contradiction the rhythm of Peace or Harmony reveals beauty, unity, and order in the universe. Further in the spiritual evolution of man, life and matter are not opposed to each other, as the Infinite manifests itself through the unanimity of the many. The more we realize this Peace or Harmony the nearer we are to the goal of evolution. On fully comprehending this unity man reaches the goal of evolution (the development of the inner consciousness) and becomes one with the Infinite.

Bliss is the equanimity towards which the prayer of man's heart ever rises throughout the ages mysteriously and consciously. In Hinduism, the Absolute or the Ultimate Reality is conceived as pervading the universe. It is the goal of the Hindu to attain, by personal experience through direct revelation, some understanding of the essential Being of the Absolute, who is beyond all material forms and consists of knowledge and bliss.

While, Non-Dual means, "the realization of that oneness in the soul which through all disruption and dissention continues to establish relationships in joy and love."[3]

Therefore, the Ultimate Reality, according to Tagore is one, infinite, eternal spirit whose nature is essentially peaceful, blissful and Non-Dual. Shankaracharya, the famous exponent of the Advaita School of Vedanta preached that there is only one true reality (*Brahman*) which is the source of everything and all differentiations and pluralities are illusory. He regards Brahman as real and the Universe as only *Maya* or unreal. We perceive many things in the universe under the influence of *Maya,* but the reality is only one. However, Tagore unlike Shankaracharya does not regard the innumerable passing things as unreal, they are as much real as the one.

Tagore explains the nature of the Reality as being a synthesis of the Infinite-Finite relationship. To him, Infinite is the Reality's essence and Finite is its manifestation. Tagore quotes two important verses of the *Isha Upanishad* in his book *Personality*[4] which support his faith in the unity of the Infinite and the finite in reality. It is stated in that *Upanishad* that one who has the knowledge of the finite and the Infinite both crosses the sea of death and ultimately attains immortality. Mere knowledge of the finite is as dangerous as that of the infinite. One should, therefore, combine the two.

The enigma of the relationship between the infinite and the finite occupies a central place in Tagore's ideology. Man is a finite-infinite being. He is finite if we view him as a body or mind, but he is infinite, as a soul. Man combines in him spirit and nature. He is earth's child but heaven's inheritor. According to Tagore, the self (*atman*) has two aspects—finite and infinite. In the finite pole, the self maintains its own unique individuality in the universe. Each individual has a distinct personality; and it is owing to this uniqueness of personality that each individual possesses a distinct being in the universe. He has a being and value of his own. Tagore points out that if this individuality is annihilated, then though no material is lost, the creative joy which was crystallized therein is gone. He is absolutely ruined if he is deprived of this speciality or individuality, which is the only thing he can call his own; which, if lost, is a loss to the whole world.[5] For example, in *Chitra*, Chitra has a specific individuality. She is captivated by Arjuna but Arjuna is not at all impressed by her personality and therefore in order to enamour Arjuna, Chitra destroys her distinct personality and having been blessed by the god of Love and god of Spring, she transforms herself as a beautiful, delicate damsel. She succeeds in winning Arjuna but in time she realizes that something is wrong somewhere. She realizes that Arjuna does not love her and that he loves her physical beauty which in reality, is a borrowed one. Arjuna loves the unreal (Illusion) and not the real. Consequently, she is disheartened and disillusioned. She says:

> Surely this cannot be love, this is not man's highest homage to woman! Alas, that this frail disguise, the body, should make one blind to the light of the deathless spirit![6]

Chitra contemplates giving up the frail disguise that she has enwrapped herself in. She says:

> I will reveal my true self to him, a nobler thing than this disguise.[7]

Subsequently, Chitra comprehends that the creative joy, which was crystallized in her, has gone. Further, when Arjuna also feels that something is missing in his life, he thinks that he has forgotten his real self as the Kshatriya Prince, the vigorous, powerful, dutiful warrior and loving brother. At that moment he states:

> Give me something to clasp, something that can last longer than pleasure, that can endure even through suffering.[8]

Chitra, then, immediately realizes that the reason for which she has obtained the blessing of beauty from the gods has been shattered. She understands that Arjuna is no longer infatuated. On the contrary he has developed a liking for the Other Chitra, the huntress, which essentially was her true self. He says:

> Illusion is the first appearance of Truth. She advances towards her lover in disguise. But a time comes when she throws off her ornaments and veils and stands clothed in naked dignity. I grope for that ultimate you, the bare simplicity of truth.[9]

To Tagore, the relationship between the Finite and the Infinite is one of codependence. The Infinite manifests itself through the Finite and the Finite finds its realization in the Infinite. Tagore says:

> The Infinite for its self-expression, comes down into the manifoldness of the finite; and the finite, for its self-realization must rise into the unity of the Infinite. Than only is the Cycle of Truth complete.[10]

The Finite and the Infinite are whole in their union. Without the finite the eternal love drama comes to a standstill. Tagore believes it to be a game of hide and seek. The most remarkable point to be observed here is that in this game, the finite realizes the infinite through separation and union. Tagore sings:

> The child finds its mother when it leaves her womb[...].[11]

Often, the Finite self finds himself alienated from the Infinite and feels like a fish out of water. The Finite then yearns for union with the Infinite. Similarly, after having realized the Truth, Chitra and Arjuna yearn for higher love. They ascend from the physical to the spiritual.

Further, the relationship between the individual and the universe is not one of conflict and enmity, but one of harmony and love, and the realization of this unity is the highest goal of life. In Tagore, the Finite (the stream of Becoming) is continually seeking to identify itself with Infinite (the sea of Being).

Tagore propounds that Man's goal is the realization of the supreme Person, the Infinite, seated in the lotus of our heart. To realize our oneness with the Supreme Being is the highest aim of our life. This is our *dharma.* Man's *dharma* is to become the Infinite, which he essentially is. He states:

> Religion consists in the endeavour of men to cultivate and express those qualities which are inherent in the nature of Man the eternal, and to have faith in him.[12]

In *Chitra*, both Chitra and Arjuna strive to attain the stage of higher love after having realized that true love is beyond the physical self.

To Tagore, there are two methods of realizing the goal of life. The first is that one should visualize Nature as living and endeavour to establish a contact with her, while the other is Love that leads to the Infinite. It is through the intensifying of our consciousness into love, and extending it to the world, that we can experience this infinite joy.

Tagore believes that man's salvation lies in his freeing his personality from the narrow limitations of the ego or the little self. The ego or the little self makes us forget our true being. In our selfishness and ignorance we believe that the path to blessedness lies in the possession of riches, but our needs are not satisfied by what we acquire. The real misery or ignorance of man is that he has not fully come out of the dark chamber of the little self. It is only after one has defeated the ego or the little self that true love emerges, which ultimately leads to salvation. Tagore's *Chitra* grows to be free from the yoke of the ego or the little self. Her egoless love springs out in the ninth scene. She says:

> The gift that I proudly bring you is the heart of a woman. Here have all pains and joys gathered, the hopes and fears and shames of a daughter of the dust; here love springs up struggling towards immortal life.[13]

Tagore correspondingly opines in *Sadhana*:

> Therefore love is the highest bliss [...], that man can attain to, for through it alone he truly knows that he is more than himself, and that he is at one with the All.[14]

In *Chitra* Tagore proposes that the acquired beauty of Chitra is fundamentally transient in nature. And such procured beauty is devoid of either physical satisfaction or spiritual contentment. Chitra's attempt to acquire Arjuna's love is therefore an exercise in futility on account of her lack of knowledge. Tagore says:

> Avidya is the ignorance that darkens our consciousness, and tends to limit it within the boundaries of our personal self [...]. So, when a man leaves the life of Avidya he is confined within his own self. It is a spiritual sleep; his consciousness is not fully awake to the highest reality that surrounds him, therefore he knows not the reality of his own soul.[15]

Thus, Chitra's lack of knowledge or *Avidya* becomes the cause that prevents her from attaining to a higher state of being or consciousness.

Secondly, Tagore is of the opinion that Man has to come out of the narrow self for the further play of his greater Self. His heart has to vibrate with the music of the eternal, and live the life of goodness and to live the life of goodness is to live the life of All. Goodness lies in the expansion of the self and this expansion alone can save mankind from the labyrinth of evil and suffering. Man's deepest joy is in growing greater and greater by more and more union with the All. The supreme spiritual ideal of man is to enlarge his field of consciousness over the entire world.

Further, Tagore distinguishes between the individual's wish and will. An individual has got only wish when he is selfish and narrow-minded. But he is said to have will when he is broad-minded. This will (but not wish) is in accordance with the universal will.[16]

Man's true freedom lies in the growth of personality from the life of the flesh to the life of the spirit. An individual's growth finds its supreme expression in the divinity of 'Man—the Eternal.' Repeatedly, Tagore dwells on love. It is through love that one transcends the barriers built by the limited self and realizes the deeper affinity with the All. Love is the outcome of detachment from our egoistic self and of broadening our field of consciousness towards higher and larger spheres. When we attain to that higher and larger self, we are released from the bonds of pain and pleasure, and the place vacated by our narrow self becomes filled with an abounding joy springing from measureless love. Tagore says:

> Joy is the realization of the truth of oneness, the oneness of our soul with the world and of the world-soul with the supreme lover.[17]

This is the attainment of true mystical illumination or what Tagore would like to call *Brahma-Vihara*—living in the Infinite or the revelation of the Infinite—in us. And when a man attains the state of *Brahma-Vihara,* he sings out of joy:

> The inward and the outward has become as one sky,
> The infinite and the finite are united.
> I am drunken with the sight of this All.[18]

Truly speaking, the state *of Brahma-Vihara* is the revelation of the Infinite. Thus, inner transformation of man is the remedy suggested by Tagore in resolving the contraries of life in *Chitra.*

4.1 The Philosophy of Aurobindo in *Savitri*

Aurobindo, like Tagore, is essentially a mystic poet. His poetry is concerned with the exploration of the Life Divine and with the revelation of the Real and the True. Like all great poetry, it is lighted up with a divine fire. Aurobindo thoughtfully reveals the divine spirit in a human body of the Super-Mind. God, the World-Mother, the Universe and Man—all these manifestations are viewed with a mystic's vision in Aurobindo's poetry.

Aurobindo stands out as the originator of a new *Vedic* and *Upanishadic* age of poetry. *Savitri* is *Mantric* and philosophical throughout. According to K.D. Sethna:

> *Savitri* is from every angle the right correlate to the practical drive towards earth-transformation by India's mightiest Master of spirituality in his ashram at Pondicherry.[19]

Aurobindo has made a passion of the spiritual life. Our *Vedic* poets always looked beyond humanity, beyond earth and therefore they could create divine poetry. They were majestic and sublime and substantial and therefore they unaffectedly dealt with the heroic form. Aurobindo has the same outlook and this explains the ring of the old world-manner that we find in him. The Hindu legends and myths delighted him because they are always ennobling in effect. His concern was with the divine being, who is "at once our supreme transcendent Self, the Cosmic Being, the foundation of our universality, and the divinity within which our psychic being, the true evolving individual in our nature, is a portion, a spark, a flame, growing into the eternal fire from which it was lit [...]."[20]

Aurobindo made poetry a medium of articulating his positive philosophy of evolution of the human race. He held that poetry springs from a higher region. In executing his job, the poet becomes the seer and reveals to man his eternal self and the godheads of its manifestations. In other words, the true creator of poetry is the soul; in Eternity poetry begins, in Eternity it ends. In fact, Aurobindo has spoken of four levels of being between the Mental and the Highest consciousness, in the order of their ascending spiritual brilliance, and they are the *Higher Mind, Illumined Mind, Intuitive Mind,* and *Over Mind,* each producing poetry of its own particular fervour.

Aurobindo wanted poetry to be *Mantric* and Mystical. He believed that poetry must combine the following three elements:

(i) The highest intensity of rhythmic movement.

(ii) The highest intensity of style—of verbal form and thought substance.

(iii) The highest intensity of the soul's vision of Truth.

R.K. Singh explains the poetic purpose of Aurobindo in the following words:

> Aurobindo propounds that the purpose of poetry is not to teach or preach or serve any ethical aim but to

> embody beauty in the world and give delight. The creation of a new image or symbol, which is just, beautiful, meaningful and suggestive is itself a joy to the poet and the reader; his fiction is the real reality experienced in the innermost spirit. The Savitri-Satyavan legend, which articulates social and community values rather than finely differentiated individual values, by its very shape, creates a potent image. The verse is filled with the beauty and power of thought and its emotion, a rhythmic voice of life. The legend and the symbol open to deeper meanings interpretative of the multifaceted realities, voicing the oneness and totality of our being, Nature, universe and God, and thereby enriching the actuality of our earthly life. The earth life is made more beautiful with the widened realms of the soul, the intimate living with nature and its spirit. The motif of bringing God into the earth-life actually adds to and enlarges the earth-life itself, without ever negating the living and striving present or discarding the past. The narrative world reveals the beauty and order of the Universe.[21]

An indepth-study of *Savitri* brings to the fore the philosophy of Aurobindo, which inherently is in line with the ancient *rishis* and sages of India. That God envelops the universe is a recurrent *Upanishadic* idea in Aurobindo's *Savitri*. Aurobindo says that God—the Absolute is the essential reality of our existence. It is indeterminate and incomprehensible but is generally recognized by immortal souls as Existence, Consciousness and Bliss. *Savitri* reveals that Existence is the omnipresent reality. It is pure, indefinable, infinite and absolute. It is a static being; but it causes the movements of Becoming. The *Isha Upanishad* states:

> It moves and It moves not; It is far and near; It is within all this and It is also outside all this.[22]

In *The Life Divine*, Aurobindo says that Existence is really the substratum of Becoming:

> The very conception of movement carries with it the potentiality of repose and betrays itself as an activity of some existence; the very idea of energy in action

> carries with it the idea of energy abstaining from action; and an absolute energy not in action is simply and purely absolute existence.[23]

Existence is basically indefinite. *The Svetashvatara Upanishad* calls it "without parts, without activity, tranquil, irreproachable, without blemish."[24]

It has two aspects—the indeterminate (*Nirguna*) and the determinate (*Saguna*). For Shankara, existence is the indeterminate; for Ramanujan, it is the determinate. But Aurobindo believes that existence is both indeterminate and determinate (*Nirguna* and *Saguna*) simultaneously.

Further, the Absolute possesses Force, but it is not subject to Force. It manifests itself as force in both its immovable (static) and vigorous (dynamic) aspects and at the same time transcends both the aspects. Aurobindo believes that this Force is conscious; for the phenomena of consciousness cannot come about from unconscious force. Unlike the materialists Aurobindo holds that matter itself is the form of Consciousness-Force. *Savitri* reveals that Absolute, which creates the cosmos out of Its Consciousness-Force is:

> The Absolute, the Perfect, the Alone
> Has called out of the Silence his mute Force
> Where she lay in the featureless and formless hush
> Guarding from Time by her immobile sleep
> The ineffable puissance of his solitude
> The Absolute, the Perfect, the Alone
> Has entered with his silence into space;
> He has fashioned these countless persons of one self;
> He lives in all, who lived in his vast alone;
> Space is himself and Time is only he.
> The Absolute, the Perfect, the Immune,
> One who is in us as our secret self,
> Our mask of imperfection has assumed,
> He has made this tenement of flesh his own,
> His image in the human measure cast,
> That to his divine measure we might rise
> Than in a figure of divinity [...].[25]

Existence manifests itself in relation to the universe in three aspects: *Atman* (self), *Purusha* (spirit) and *Ishwara* (God).

Similarly, Consciousness-Force appears as *Maya, Prakriti* and *Shakti* (in complete correspondence to the three aspects of existence). The Absolute expresses itself as the *atman* of all existence. In Hinduism *atman,* is the term for the breath or the soul and principle of life. The *atman*, or personal or individual soul, however, is believed to be identical with *Brahman* (*Aatma so Paramatma*), the universal world soul, or godhead. In Hindu philosophy, the term *atman* also indicates the true essence of anything, together with the universe. The *atman* is said to be the only thing that truly exists, an immortal substance that transmigrates from body to body. And *Maya* is said to be the self-power (*atma-shakti*) of *atman.* It is only through *Maya* that *atman* creates itself into many forms (*Ekoham Bahusyam*). Aurobindo says:

> He whose transcendence rules the pregnant Vasts,
> Prescient now dwells in our subliminal depths,
> A Luminous individual Power, alone.[26]

According to *Vedantic* ideology, the idea that the world is a multiplicity of distinct things is considered *maya,* or an illusion, resulting from the conventional way of thinking. Since *maya* has the original meaning of "to measure," the world is thought to be measured or marked out by those divisions and classifications of human experience that words and ideas make possible. To describe a convoluted arch, one must measure it as if it were a series of distinct points. Similarly, to describe and think about nature, one must break it up into controllable units or terms, that is, things and events. This procedure, however useful, gives the strong impression that events are separable from one another, that one could happen without another, and that pleasure could exist without pain or life without death. A similar impression prevails concerning the separability of things. The central problem in Shankara's system of interpretation is the nature of the relation between *Brahman* and *atman,* the individual self, breath, or soul. According to Shankara, the two are identical. *Avidya,* or ignorance, however, prevents the individual self from understanding the non-dual universal nature of *Brahman.* Thus it perceives only separate selves and things (that is, the whole world of material, temporal existence), and never realizes that all separate existences are in essence unreal (these being phenomena produced by *maya*, the power of illusion mysteriously inherent in and projected from Brahman). As long as the individual self remains without real knowledge, it will blindly look for its true self in the phenomenal world. It remains enmeshed in that world, again and again experiencing *samsara*, or the series of existences, deaths, and rebirths each unenlightened soul undergoes as a consequence of its *karma* (its good and evil actions in past existences, which determine the form of future existences). Through the proper knowledge of *Vedanta*, however, the individual soul recognizes the limitless reality forever existing behind the cosmic veil of *maya*, realizes that its own true nature is identical with Brahman (*Aatmaiva Brahma*), and through this self-realization achieves *moksha* (release from *samsara* and *karma)* and *Nirvana*.

Purusha, the second aspect of existence, is said to be the Conscious-Being of the Absolute and *prakriti* is said to be its Consciousness-Force. The Spirit (*Purusha*) and matter or nature (*Prakriti*), which is divided into the triple strands of goodness, passion, and darkness, is complementary. *Purusha* and *Prakriti* are intimately related to each other. In fact *Purusa* supports *Prakriti:*

> In a thousand ways he serves her royal needs;
> He makes the hours pivot around her will,
> Makes all reflect her whims; all is their play:
> This whole wide world is only he and she [...].
> The Two who are one are the secret of all power,
> The Two who are one are the might and right in things
> His soul, silent, supports the world and her,
> His acts are her commandment's registers.[27]

Purusha also enjoys the works of *Prakriti* and becomes what she wants him to be:

> He feels the sweetness of her mastering touch, [...].
> He revels in her, a swimmer in her sea, [...].
> He rejoices in her every thought and act
> And gives consent to all that she can wish,
> Whatever she desires he wills to be
> The Spirit, the innumerable One [...].[28]

Aurobindo's conception of *Purusha* and *Prakriti* differs from that of Sankhya philosophy. The Sankhya school of philosophy says that *Purusha* and *Prakriti* are two distinct entities. *Purusha* is conscious but inactive, while *Prakriti* is active but unconscious. However Aurobindo thinks that *Purusa* and *Prakriti* are essentially one. The *Prakriti* may be apparently inconscient; but it conceals a secret consciousness. Similarly *Purusha* appears to be led by *Prakriti;* but in reality *Purusha* controls *Prakriti* because he is his own *Prakriti.*

In alternation, *Ishwara* is recognised as the Lord of creation. He is both individual beings and the underlying reality of the universe. And *Shakti* is itself the power of *Ishwara.* Every male god is said to have his *shakti,* the embodiment of his own potencies, expressed through his consort; and every human being has a *shakti,* although women have more than men. (The name *Shakti* is used for the supreme goddess herself, said to have been created by the merging of all the powers (*shaktees*) emitted by the male gods, who needed her to kill the buffalo demon *Mahisha*).

Thus, in the first aspect of Reality, *Purusha* creates *Prakriti* out of His *maya.* In the second aspect, *Purusha* does what *Prakriti* wants him to do. In these two aspects, Reality is not perceived in any definite form. But in the third aspect Reality is openly seen. There he is the Lord of his *Shakti* and of all things.

> He is the substance, he is the self of things,
> She has forged from him her works of skill and might: [...]
> Ever he repeats his ceaseless births.
> He is the Maker and the world he made,
> He is the vision and he is the seer;
> He is himself the actor and the act
> He is himself the knower and the known,
> He is himself the dreamer and the dream.
> There are Two who are One and play in many worlds;
> In Knowledge and Ignorance they have spoken and met
> And light and darkness are there eyes' interchanged.[29]

Bliss is the third attribute of the Absolute. It is for bliss and out of bliss that the Absolute creates the world. The soul is said to be the eternal portion of bliss. Shankaracharya also says, *Chidanandarupah shivoham shivoham.*[30] The presence of pain and suffering does not contradict the universality of bliss. Even pain and suffering hide a kind of bliss:

> Bliss is the secret stuff of all that lives,
> Even pain and grief are garbs of world-delight,
> It hides behind thy sorrow and thy cry.[31]

The Taittiriya Upanishad affirms that Brahman is bliss:

> He knew that Brahman is bliss. For truly, beings here are born from bliss, when born, they live by bliss and into bliss, when departing, they enter.[32]

When all-consciousness descends into mental consciousness, he assumes the form of Ignorance. It is ignorance that causes sorrows and sufferings. Aurobindo believes that all-consciousness assumes the mask of ignorance to transform ignorance into knowledge. The Absolute becomes human to make human divine. He descends through Existence-Consciousness-Bliss and also through the medium of the supermind into the overmind, mind, psyche, life, matter and the inconscient. Therefore, in the manifestation, Existence becomes matter; Consciousness becomes life; Bliss becomes the psyche and the Supermind becomes the mind.

D.S. Mishra briefly sums up the philosophy of Aurobindo in the following words:

> *Savitri* reveals that the universe is really a double process of descent and ascent. The Absolute descends through Existence-Consciousness-Force-Bliss and also through the medium of the Supermind to mind, life, matter and the inconscient. The Spirit involved in the inconscient, in return, has evolved the principles of matter, life and mind and it is destined to manifest the Supermind in the course of time. Furthermore, *Savitri* reveals that a liberated soul should not aspire to merge his consciousness into the Absolute nor should he choose to enter into the heaven of everlasting day. He must, after realizing the highest consciousness, come down to work for the supramentalisation of man and matter.[33]

According to Aurobindo:

> Spirit evolved into the inconscient and it is evolving itself slowly into different forms to establish the life

> divine on earth. Therefore, the physical world might be described as the evolution of involved spirit. The process of evolution, it is said, follows a triple character: a widening, a heightening and an integration. When evolution starts, the forms of matter proceed from the simple to more complex forms. This process is called 'widening.' Heightening is a process in which the forms of the lower grade move to the higher grade. When the evolution reaches a higher grade it takes up all the lower grades and transforms them in the light of its own principles. Thus, there is not merely an ascent from a lower to the higher grade; but there is the transformation of the lower grades as well. This is known as the process of integration [...].
>
> What is necessary is a working that brings the lower gradation of being to a point at which the higher can manifest in it; at that point a pressure from some superior plane where the new power is dominant may assist [...]. It is in some such way that the transition from the lower to the higher grades of consciousness seems to have been made in nature.[34]

This is precisely what *Savitri* sets out to do. *Savitri* in fact lays bare the process of spiritual evolution. The ideas of evolution have also formed an important segment in western philosophy. Plato refers to it in his *Timaeus* (The treatise embodies a theory of the universe). For Aristotle, evolution is the gradual transformation of the potential into the actual. In his metaphysical theory, Aristotle criticized Plato's separation of form from matter and maintained that the Forms, or essences, are contained within the concrete objects that exemplify them. Everything real, for Aristotle, is a combination of potentiality and actuality.[35]

But the theory of evolution can be explained from different points of view in the nineteenth century. Darwin thinks that evolution is a mechanical process; it is the progressive adjustment of the individual with his environment. The scientific development that most affected ethics after the time of Newton was the theory of evolution advanced by Charles Darwin. Darwin's findings provided documentary support for the system, sometimes termed evolutionary ethics, propounded by the British philosopher Herbert Spencer, according to whom morality is merely the result of certain habits acquired by humanity in the course of evolution. A startling but logical elaboration of the Darwinian thesis that survival of the fittest is a basic law of nature was advanced by the German philosopher Friedrich Nietzsche, who held that so-called moral conduct is necessary only for the weak. Moral conduct—especially such as was advocated in Jewish and Christian ethics, which in his view is a slave ethic—tends to allow the weak to inhibit the self-realization of the strong. According to Nietzsche, every action should be directed toward the development of the superior individual, or *Übermensch* ("superman"), who will be able to realize the noblest possibilities of life. Nietzsche found this ideal individual exemplified in the persons of ancient Greek philosophers before Plato and of military dictators such as Julius Caesar and Napoleon.[36]

The German philosopher G.W.F. Hegel applied the term to his own philosophic system, based on the idealistic concept of a universal mind that, through evolution, seeks to arrive at the highest level of self-awareness and freedom. The so-called dialectical materialism of Karl Marx, often considered a revision of the Hegelian system, asserts that the material or objective universe exists independently of mind, which is a reflection of material reality. Hegel considers evolution to be spiritual in the sense that it is the gradual unfoldment of the universal reason in matter, life and mind.[37]

Henri Bergson, the noted French philosopher and Nobel laureate, also advanced a theory of evolution, based on the spiritual dimension of human life. He is of the opinion that the creator has no control over the creation. Besides the creator knows nothing about the end of creation. Just as a painter does not have a fore-knowledge of a finished portrait, so too the creator does not have a final picture of the end of the world.[38]

Aurobindo agrees with none of these thinkers. To him evolution is spiritual in the sense that it is the Spirit's return to itself. Evolution is thus the home-coming of the Spirit. So philosophically *Savitri* stresses that men are not essentially a heap of broken images; they are really the sons of God, (*amritasya putraha*). Of course, at this stage of evolution, they are certainly the victims of fate. Nonetheless, they are free to mould their destiny by the strength of their soul. They have a divine spark, a psychic being within themselves. If they bring it to the force to govern their mind, life and body they will be able to attain knowledge, power and bliss. To discover their soul, they must reject the temptations of the lower nature and surrender themselves to the divine mother.

Aurobindo's *Savitri* primarily concentrates on the evolution of the human soul. However there is the impediment of Death in the form of Ignorance that often prevents man from realizing his true identity. It is here that *Savitri* succeeds and establishes a new order and scheme of things for the entire human race. Thus it is important that we first comprehend what constitutes the nature of Death.

The Ideas about death vary with different cultures and in different epochs. In Western societies, death has traditionally been seen as the departure of the soul from the body. In this tradition, the essence of being human is independent of physical properties. Since the soul has no corporeal manifestation, its departure cannot be seen or otherwise objectively determined. Hence, in this tradition, the cessation of breathing has been taken as the sign of death. However, *Savitri* is destined to destroy Death in order to bring about the immortality of man. Most of the Vedic seers and sages believe that the body is mortal while the soul is immortal. If one realizes one's soul, one becomes immortal. However this realization takes place only when one identifies and unites with the Absolute. This happens only when one shakes off one's body in death and the spirit is released to go to the world of the immortals. Death is thus a path from mortality to immortality. Savitri also shows that death is a door to eternity:

> Death is a stair, a door, a stumbling stride
> The soul must take to cross from birth to birth,
> A grey defeat pregnant with victory,
> A whip to lash us towards our breathless state.
> The inconscient world is the spirit's self-made room,
> Eternal Night shadow of eternal day.[39]

The doctrine of immortality is common to many religions; in different cultures, however, it takes various forms, ranging from ultimate extinction of the soul to its final survival and the resurrection of the body. In Hinduism, the ultimate personal goal is considered absorption into the "universal spirit" (*Moksha*). The Buddhist doctrine promises *nirvana,* the state of complete bliss achieved through total extinction of the personality. In the religion of ancient Egypt, entrance to immortal life was dependent on the results of divine examination of the merits of an individual's life. Early Greek religion promised a shadowy continuation of life on earth in an underground region known as Hades. In Christianity and Islam, as well as in Judaism, the immortality promised is primarily of the spirit. The former two religions both differ from Judaism in holding that after the resurrection of the body and a general judgment of the entire human race, the body is to be reunited with the spirit to experience either reward or punishment. According to the Jewish belief, the resurrection of the soul will take place at the advent of the Messiah, although the reunion of body and spirit will endure only for the messianic age, when the spirit will return to heaven.[40] For the *Upanishadic* sages, immortality is the realization of *atman* (self). If one knows *atman,* one knows everything. *The Katha Upanishad* states:

> He who knows this self, experiences it, as the living spirit, close at hand, as the lord of the past and the future, does not shrink away from him. This verily is that.[41]

The Hindu literature has in fact a complex cosmology. The Hindus believe that the universe is a great, enclosed sphere, a cosmic egg, within which are numerous concentric heavens, hells, oceans, and continents, with India at the center. They believe that time is both degenerative—going from the golden age, or *Krita Yuga,* through two intermediate periods of decreasing goodness, to the present age, *or Kali Yuga*—and cyclic: at the end of each *Kali Yuga,* the universe is destroyed by fire and flood, and a new golden age begins. Human life, too, is cyclic: After death, the soul leaves the body and is reborn in the body of another person, animal, vegetable, or mineral. This process of endless entanglement in activity and rebirth is called *samsara.* The precise quality of the new birth is determined by the accumulated merit and demerit that result from all the actions, or *karma,* that the soul has committed in its past life or lives. All Hindus believe that *karma* accumulates in this way; they also believe, however, that it can be counteracted by expiations and rituals, by "working out" through punishment or reward, and by achieving release (*moksha*) from the entire process of *samsara* through the renunciation of all worldly desires. *The Bhagvad Gita* states:

> Karmanyevadhikarste ma phaleshu, kadachan
> Ma karmaphalaheturbhuh ma te sangostvakarmani.[42]

It teaches us the principle of disinterested action that does not cause bondage. It stresses that one must perform one's allotted duty without taking any interest in the result of one's action. Further, if a person is devotional, he should surrender himself to the supreme, and take refuge only in him. Finally, the *Bhagavat Gita* states the various ways of achieving liberation for the people of different temperaments. Aurobindo, however, says that the Gita teaches us to perform the divine action for self-perfection.[43]

Shankaracharya, the most famous exponent of the *Advaita Vedanta* school of philosophy, preached that there is only one true reality (*Brahman*) which is the source of everything and all differentiations and pluralities are illusory. He expounded the idea of *Jivanmukti* (liberation in life). According to him, immortality consists in recognising one's own self as non-different from *Brahman.* The Vaishnava *Vedantists* believe in *Karmamukti.* For them liberation is a spiritual pilgrimage to *Brahmaloka.* In the Sankhya Yoga, this final stage, can rarely be attained in one lifetime. Usually, several births are required to achieve liberation, first from the world of phenomena, then from thoughts of self, and finally from the spirit's entanglement with matter. The separation of spirit from matter is *Kaivalya,* or true liberation. As an adept Yogi approaches *Kaivalya,* he is supposed to acquire certain remarkable capacities. He becomes insensible to heat or cold, to injury, to pleasure or pain. He can perform supernatural, mental and physical feats and even change the course of nature. He can distinguish the subtlest elements of matter and can, at the same time, see the universe as a whole, comprehending both microcosm and macrocosm in the same thought. This school of thought also emphasizes both on *Jivanmukti* and *Videhmukti.* After the realization of discriminative knowledge (*Viveka*) the *Purusha* remains embodied for a while to exhaust the *prarabdha karmas*, just like the wheel of the potter revolves for a while due to the previous momentum, even after the potter ceases to move it. When the *prarabdha karmas* are exhausted by experiencing them, the *Purusha* gives up the body and attains the eternal (*Kaivalyam*).[44]

Aurobindo believes that immortality will be one of the possible results of the Supramentalisation. Immorality here does not mean the annihilation or cessation of physical death. It implies to live in the divine and to have divine consciousness. In other words, immortality is the realisation of one's identity with the Supreme God. This concept is no different from the *Upanishadic* idea that the realisation of one's soul is necessary for one's liberation from the cycle of births and deaths. And it is precisely here that the Yoga of *Savitri* becomes important. Savitri desiccates her physical, vital, mental desires and achieves self-restraint. She goes deep in her heart through meditation and contemplation. This could be seen as a form of self-denial and renunciation of worldly pleasure in order to attain a higher degree of spirituality, intellectuality, or self-awareness. She gradually witnesses evolution from matter to mind:

> This mind no silence knows nor dreamless sleep,
> In the incessant circling of its steps
> Thoughts trade forever through the listening brain;
> It toils like a machine and cannot stop.[45]

However, Savitri encounters three universal energies, the Mother of Sorrows, the Mother of Might and the Mother of Light. Each one of them tells Savitri that she is Savitri's soul. But Savitri only partly identifies herself with them. She knows that they are imperfect typical beings. The Mother of Sorrows is without the divine strength to prevent cruelty and violence in the world; the Mother of Might does not possess divine knowledge and therefore Savitri promises to assist them after self-realization.

Consequently, Savitri moves from one inner country to another (*Chakras*) in search of her soul. It is finally following the passage of *agni chakra* that she enters the chamber of flame and light and meets her immortal soul:

> Then through a tunnel dug in the last rock
> She came out where there shone a deathless sun.
> A house was there all made of flame and light
> And crossing a wall of doorless living fire
> There suddenly she met her secret soul.[46]

In the East, belief in a human soul is central to several philosophical and religious systems. Thus, for instance, in early Hinduism the soul or self (*atman*) was considered the principle that controls all activities and defines one's self-identity and consciousness. Aurobindo similarly says that the soul, is a spark of the divine fire that grows behind the mental, vital and physical desires of the psychic being. It is a subliminal psychic entity, which differs from the desire soul. On the other hand Tagore explains the finding of the soul in terms of moral and spiritual values:

> Therefore the realisation of our soul has its moral and spiritual side. The moral side represents the training of unselfishness, control of desire; the spiritual side represents sympathy and love. They should be taken together and never separated [...].[47]

The realisation of the soul is the first and the foremost step of Integral Yoga, for it alone can transform the physical being into gnostic being. Aurobindo states:

> But for such vast spiritual change to be,
> Out of the mystic cavern in man's heart
> The heavenly Psyche must put off her veil,
> And step into common nature's crowded rooms
> And stand uncovered in that nature's front
> And rule its thoughts and fill the body and life.[48]

It appears that Aurobindo has been influenced by the *Katha Upanishad*, wherein Yama explains the secret of life to Nachiketa. In order to secure his spiritual interests, Vajashrava performs *Vishvajit yagya* and for that he offers gifts to his people but the gifts are unworthy. This hurts the son—Nachiketa. He wants to save his father from this sin. He asks:

'O Sir, to whom wilt thou give me?' He repeats thrice and in anger his father replies, 'unto death shall I give thee.' Obeying his father's order he goes to the House of Death. He waits for three nights before Death returns and shows him hospitality due to a guest. When Yama returns and sees the boy standing at his doors, he says, 'since thou a venerable guest, hast stayed in my house without food for three nights, I make obesiance to thee, O Brahmana, May it be well with me. Therefore, in return, choose thou three gifts.' In this way, Nachiketa is granted three boons. He says:

1. That Gautama (my father) with allayed anxiety, with anger gone, may be gracious to me, O Death, and recognizing me, greet me, when set free by you and this, I choose as the first gift to the three.
2. Thou knowest, O Death, that fire (sacrifice) which is the aid to heaven. Describe it to me full of faith how the dwellers in heaven gain immortality. This I choose as my second boon.
3. There is this doubt in regard to a man who has departed, some (holding) that he is and some that he is not. I would be instructed by thee in this knowledge. Of the boons, this is the third boon.

Nachiketa's third request is specially relevant for the period after Liberation, as some systems do not accept even the separate existence of souls after Liberation, while some accept equality of the souls with God after it. Yama congratulates Nachiketa on his steadfastness in obtaining sacred knowledge and sets the distinction between *shreyas* and *preyas*—the Good and the Pleasant. Normal worldly interests such as family, property, etc., constitute the second category, while interest in God is the first. Yama expresses his happiness that Nachiketa has chosen *shreyas.* Yama makes it clear that God knowledge cannot be obtained only by logic or learning the scriptures. It is God who chooses the deserving and gives them His vision. The statement *yameva eshha vrinute,* embodying this principle of God choosing His devotee for revealing Himself, is the cornerstone of Theism and Bhakti. It is clear from this that the Upanishads do not profess Absolutism, but support Theism. The reference to *prasaada* (grace) in the expression *prasiidati* may be noted in this connection. The rest of the Upanishad is an excellent exposition of the nature of God, the fact of His being a regulator after death and Liberation, necessity of controlling the senses and the methodology of Yoga.[49]

There is unmistakably a strong parallel between the dialogue that ensues between the god of Death and Nachiketa *vis-a-vis* the god of Death and Savitri. The Mother in the referred context rightly says:

> *Savitri* is a revelation. It is a meditation, it is a quest of the Infinite, the Eternal [...]. To read *Savitri* is indeed to practise Yoga, spiritual concentration. One can find there all that is needed to realize the Divine. Each step of Yoga is found there, including the secret of all other Yogas also [...]. Each verse of *Savitri* is like a revealed Mantra and I repeat this. The words are expressed and arranged in such a way that the sonority of the rhythm leads to the original sound which is OM.[50]

Savitri deals with the riddles of faith and free will. It shows that man is a victim of fate: at the same time it stresses that man has a free will to mould his fate. *Savitri* emphasizes that fate is not the ultimate reality. Man has in himself the power to mould or modify his fate. Free will is essentially power or ability of the human mind to choose a course of action or make a decision without being subject to restraints imposed by antecedent causes, by necessity, or by divine predetermination. A completely freewill act is itself a cause and not an effect; it is beyond causal sequence or the law of causality. But at the same time the force of fate is undeniable. However the force of fate can be changed by the strength of the soul. And therefore Life is a compromise between fate and free will.[51] Aurobindo states:

> But greater spirits this balance can reverse
> And make the soul the artist of its fate.
> This is the mystic truth our ignorance hides:
> Doom is a passage for our inborn force,
> Our ordeal is the hidden spirit's choice,
> Ananke is our being's own decree.[52]

Fate is sometimes equated with the *Karma.* In Indian philosophy, the sum total of one's actions, good or bad, that are attached to the soul as it transmigrates, each new body (and each event experienced by that body) being determined by previous *karma.* The belief in *karma,* which can be traced to the *Upanishads,* is accepted by all Hindus, although they differ on many points: Some aspire to accumulate good *karma* and a good rebirth, but others, regarding all *karma* as bad, strive for release from the process of rebirth (samsara) altogether; some believe that *karma* determines all that happens to one, whereas others attribute a larger role to destiny, divine intervention, or human effort. One form of *karma* (*prarabdha*) is determined at birth and worked out in the present life; another form (*sanchita*) remains latent in this life; and a third (*sanchayamana*), gathered in this lifetime, matures in a future life.[53]

According to Buddhism, *Karma* consists of a person's acts and their ethical consequences. Human actions lead to rebirth, wherein good deeds are inevitably rewarded and evil deeds punished. Thus, neither undeserved pleasure nor unwarranted suffering exists in the world, but rather a universal justice. The karmic process operates through a kind of natural moral law rather than through a system of divine judgment. One's *karma* determines matters such as one's species, beauty, intelligence, longevity, wealth, and social status. According to Buddha, *karma* of varying types can lead to rebirth as a human, an animal, a hungry ghost, a denizen of hell, or even one of the Hindu gods. While in Jainism the fundamental doctrine consists of two eternal, coexisting, independent categories known as *jiva* (animate, living soul: the enjoyer) and *ajiva* (inanimate, non-living object: the enjoyed). The Jains believe, moreover, that the actions of mind, speech, and body produce subtle *karma* (infra-atomic particles of matter), which become the cause of bondage, and that one must eschew violence to avoid giving hurt to life. The cause of the embodiment of the soul is thought to be karmic matter; one can attain salvation (*mokhsa*) only by freeing the soul of *karma* through the practice of the three "jewels" of right faith, right knowledge, and right conduct.

Aurobindo also seems to believe in the law of *Karma.* But as a seer he visualizes that it has a limited function. Fate is in no way the sole determinant of the life of man. A man with his will power can cancel the law and the effects of *karma.* Savitri knows that Satyavan is going to die within a year and yet she marries him because she is sure that she has a soul, which will reshape her destiny. She says:

> My will is part of the eternal will,
> My fate is what my spirit's strength can make,
> My fate is what my spirit's strength can bear;
> My strength is not the titan's, it is God's.[54]

To conclude, *Savitri* is a spiritual epic and an infallible guide to awake our *aatma,* to ignite that flame in us. It helps us to reach that Ultimate, the Absolute. It will be appropriate to take recourse to the words of the Mother who says:

> Indeed *Savitri* is the supreme knowledge, above all philosophy, all religions of man. It is a spiritual way. It is *Yoga, tapasya, sadhana* everything in its single self. *Savitri* has extraordinary power; it gives out vibrations to him who can receive them—the true vibrations of each stage of consciousness. It is incomparable, it is truth in its plenitude, the truth, Sri Aurobindo brought down to earth.[55]

4.2. The Comparison between the Philosophy of Tagore and Aurobindo

1. Rabindranath Tagore and Aurobindo Ghose have drawn much of their inspiration from the Upanishads. Both of them have had mystical visions. In Tagore we find mainly two types of mysticism: Nature Mysticism and Devotional mysticism.[56] In Tagore's mysticism love (*Prema*) or joy (*Aananda*) is deep-rooted.[57] However, in Aurobindo, we find Integral mysticism. Here knowledge (*Jnana*), work (*Karma*) and Devotion (*Bhakti*) are synthesized.[58]
2. Both of them talk about the Ultimate Reality—the Absolute. Tagore refers to the Ultimate Reality as *Jivandevata*[59] or supreme Man or supreme Person,[60] or God, or Infinite, or Supreme Being, or Bridegroom or Lover.[61] While Aurobindo refers to the Ultimate Reality as *Sachchidananda*[62] or Supreme Spirit or the Infinite Person or the Lord of Creation.[63] For Tagore the Ultimate Reality is *Santam, Sivam,* and *Advaitam,*[64] whereas for

Aurobindo it is Existence, Consciousness-Force and Bliss.[65] They also talk about the personal and the impersonal aspects of Reality.

3. Both discuss about the relation between the Finite and the Infinite, which is one of interdependence. According to Tagore, the two are real in their union. He says, "Thou without me or I without thee are nothing."[66] Tagore believes that an eternal love drama takes place between the finite and the infinite. The Supreme Being requires finite individuals to enact the love-drama, for He is the eternal lover. Therefore, to Tagore, there is the eternal play of love in the relation between this being and the becoming; and in the depth of this mystery is the source of all truth and beauty that sustains the endless march of creation.[67] Similarly, Aurobindo believes that there is no such separation of them in the all-view of the Absolute.[68] Finite and Infinite are complements of each other.[69] To Aurobindo, the universe is the eternal play of the Divine *Purusha* and the Divine *Prakriti,* the immortal dance of Shiva and Kali. He calls the whole of the world-existence a *leela,* the play, the child's joy, the poet's joy, the actor's joy, the mechanician's joy of the Soul of things eternally young, perpetually inexhaustible, creating and re-creating Himself in Himself for the sheer bliss of that self-creation, of that self-representation,—Himself the play, Himself the player, Himself the playground.[70]

4. Both the philosophers talk about the goal of human life as being the oneness of the Finite and the Infinite. Tagore believes that in order to be One with the All, one must reach the summit of Consciousness called Love, as Love aims at union.[71] It is through the heightening of our consciousness into love, and extending it all over the world, that we can attain *Brahma-vihara,* communion with this infinite joy.[72] Therefore love is the highest bliss that man can attain to, for through it alone "he truly knows that he is more than himself, and that he is at one with the All."[73] Love in Tagore's mysticism is the means as well as the end.[74] Secondly an enthusiastic surrender to the spontaneity

of natural scenery leads a man to his goal.[75] To Tagore man's salvation lies in his freeing his personality from the narrow limitations of selfhood, from the narrow bigoted perspective of selfishness; his fulfilment consists in breaking the bounds of his isolated or private self and bringing himself into contact with the All,[76] as it is suggested in *Chitra*. Man must realize the wholeness of his existence, his place in the infinite.[77] This is man's destiny. Thus to him to realize our oneness with the Supreme Being is the highest aim of our life. This is our *Dharma*.[78] Aurobindo, on the other hand, believes that that Oneness can be achieved only by attaining to the Supra-consciousness. To Aurobindo, the goal of man is to attain gnostic transformation. He says, "Transfer the divided individual into the world-personality: let all thy self be divine: This is thy very goal!"[79] Thus, the aim of man is not only to attain personal salvation but the integral transformation of the whole of mankind also,[80] as it is suggested in *Savitri*.

5. Both of them discuss the problem of evil. To Tagore, "evil cannot altogether arrest the course of life on the highway and rob it of its possessions; for evil, being not a permanent fixture of the world, has to pass on, it has to grow into good, and it is possible for man to transmute it into joy, for she (evil) is the vestal virgin consecrated to the service of the immortal perfection, and when she takes her true place before the altar of the infinite she casts off her dark veil and bares her face to the beholder as a revelation of supreme joy."[81] Tagore states that only by suffering and sorrow shall you be freed from your crushing load [...]. Only by great suffering and terrible humiliation shall you be made whole.[82] Thus, evil and pain are aids to our spiritual progress. They purify the soul. It is out of love that God sends suffering. In the moments of pain and suffering, man is conscious of his moral duties and responsibilities, which indirectly help him in the path of spiritual realization. Similarly, to Aurobindo, evil is only a phase in the evolution of man. Hence, it does not form a permanent feature of the world but arises at

a certain stage (in the plane of mind) when certain conditions prevail and disappear with the disappearance of those conditions. The world as such is not evil. In the beginning when the world was evolved by the darkness of Inconscience there was no evil. So also in the end when the Superman will emerge there will be no evil. It is only in the intermediary stage which represents where we are at present that there exists any evil.[83] Aurobindo opines that as regards suffering, which is so great a stumbling block to our understanding of the universe, it is evidently a consequence of the limitation of consciousness.[84] Because to a wider outlook evil and suffering appear only as a striking aspect, they are not the whole defect.[85] However, Aurobindo states that pain and suffering can turn into their opposite, even into the original All-Delight *Aananda.*[86] This will be possible only when the supra-mental consciousness will emerge and effect a radical transformation in course of evolutionary progression.[87]

6. Both of them talk about the necessity of annihilating ego or little self or lower self or selfishness in order to attain self-realization. According to Tagore, ego-consciousness (*aham*) blurs the vision of God and makes us narrow-minded. Therefore it is in the ego-free state that one can have the vision of God. Most of the evil or suffering arrives simply because we try to live only in the individual and not in the Universal.[88] Tagore believes that when a man lives the life of *Avidya* he is confined within his own self. It is a spiritual sleep; his consciousness is not fully awake to the highest reality that surrounds him, therefore he does not know the reality of his own soul.[89] To Tagore, when a self spreads itself into all others and the selfish individual merges in the selfless universal will then only our sufferings cease, because ego is the main obstacle to salvation. He says, "I can realise the Infinite only when I have got rid of the lower self."[90] On the other hand, Aurobindo believes that when ego disappears one can participate in the life of the All. To him, the human (mental) personality can be changed into a psychic personality

only if it gets rid of all kinds of egoistic impulses and selfish desires by making a self surrender to the Divine and by making an approach to the Divine through mind, heart and will.[91] To Aurobindo, when the Over-Mind descends, the predominance of the ego-sense is entirely subordinated and finally lost, a wide feeling of a boundless universal self replaces it.[92]

7. Both reject the ascetic's denial of life and the sensualist's denial of the Spirit. Tagore does not want to be a recluse. He advocates that one should not fly away from the fever and fret of active life.[93] Tagore does not preach outward renunciation in the form of asceticism but the inner renunciation of a selfish life. He points out that the spiritual self has its enjoyment in the renunciation of the individual self for the sake of the supreme soul. This renunciation is not in the negation of the self but in the dedication of it.[94] On the contrary the world offers splendid opportunities for self-development. The world is but the progress of pilgrims in their quest for the infinite to attain eternal life here and now. He says, we are reaching him here in this very spot, now at this very moment.[95] Similarly, Aurobindo condemns *Vairagya* of the ascetic kind. He opines that the realization of the Absolute does not necessitate the denial of the world. He talks about attaining salvation 'here and now.'[96] It is not by removing himself from the world but by carrying the world with him that man can attain his goal. Aurobindo states that the gnostic evolution would only be achieved by a descent of the Super-Mind into the terrestrial formula bringing into it the supreme law and light and dynamics of the Spirit and penetrating with it and transforming the inconscience of the material basis.[97] Albert Schweitzer aptly observes that Aurobindo, "like Tagore, attempts to explain Brahmanic mysticism in the sense of [...] life affirmation."[98]

8. For Tagore the body is not the prison-house of the soul, it is the temple of the spirit, the field for spiritual growth. He says, "In your body is the garden of flowers."[99] Therefore to treat it as cheap and vulgar is equally

impious. Tagore points out, "No, I will never shut the doors of my senses. The delight of sight and hearing and touch will bear thy delight."[100] Therefore, to regard the body or any part of it as indecent is the sin of impiety. Similarly, for Aurobindo, the body is not to be neglected or condemned since divine life is possible only in this divine body. The integral yogi is required to turn the body into a temple in which the Eternal may be installed. Aurobindo states, "It can be, therefore, no integral yoga which ignores the body or makes its annulment or its rejection indispensable to a perfect spirituality. Rather, the perfecting of the body also should be the last triumph of the Spirit and to make the bodily life also divine must be God's final seal upon His work in the universe."[101] Aurobindo adds, It is no part of this Yoga to suppress taste, *rasa,* altogether. What is to be got rid of is vital desire and attachment, [...][102] Aurobindo maintains that the body is not to be neglected as it is an instrument or means of fulfilment of *Dharma*—(*Shariram Khalu Dharmasadhanam*).Our whole being—soul, mind, sense, heart, will, life, body—must consecrate all its energies so entirely and in such a way that it shall become a fit vehicle for the Divine.[103] He marks out that it is a mistake to neglect the body and let it waste away; the body is the means of *Sadhana* and should be maintained in good order. There should be no attachment to it, but no contempt or neglect either of the material part of our nature.[104] The body becomes a transparency through which the spirit shines, a glass for its indwelling flame. This is reminiscent of the conception of a radiant or luminous body, the Vedic '*Jyotirmaya deha.*' Therefore a divine life in a divine body is the formula of the ideal that we envisage.[105]

9. According to Tagore, *Avidya* is the ignorance that darkens our consciousness, and tends to limit it within the boundaries of our personal self [...]. So, when a man lives the life of *Avidya* he is confined within his own self. It is a spiritual sleep; his consciousness is not fully awake to the highest reality that surrounds him, therefore he knows not the reality of his own soul.[106]

The real misery or ignorance of man is that he has not fully come out of the dark chamber of the little self (*Aham*). Man has to come out of the little self for the fuller play of his greater self. While, the mind, according to Aurobindo, is the function of Ignorance attempting to know or it is the ignorance receiving a derivative knowledge. It is the action of *Avidya.* The Supermind is always the disclosure of an inherent and self-existent knowledge; it is the action of *vidya.*[107] The Supermind therefore is the full self-awareness of the infinite, but the mind can hardly know the Infinite in the strict sense of the term. It can at best construct highly idealised images of the Infinite. In its quest of truth the mind always proceeds piecemeal, taking snapshots of Reality from the limited standpoints.[108]

10. Both the philosophers believe in the universal will. Tagore distinguishes between the individual and the universal will.[109] An individual has got only wish when he is selfish and narrow-minded. But he is said to have will when he is broad-minded. To will properly is to consent in the universal will. Then begins the development of a truer and larger vision of life. Consequently, his perspective changes and his will takes the place of his wishes; for will is the supreme wish of the larger life. To the man who lives "for the good of humanity, life has an extensive meaning and to that extent pain becomes less important to him."[110] Similarly, Aurobindo points out that will gives the effect of self-fulfilling force. Further, he synthesizes the Consciousness of will with the Supermind Being and Consciousness of Knowledge. *Savitri* is the supreme example of the Will that Aurobindo talks about.[111]

11. There is an interesting blend, in Tagore's mysticism, of the Upanishadic concept of divine immanence with the Vaishnava concept of personal Supreme Being. R.C. Zaehner rightly observes, "Rabindranath Tagore, though he was city-bred and English-educated, owed much to his father Devendranath. From him he inherited a mysticism that was neither Advaita nor yet Bhakti, but a subtle combination of the two [...]."[112] Radhakrishnan

points out, "There are two views regarding his philosophy of life. If we believe one side, he is a Vedantin, a thinker who draws his inspiration from the Upanishads. If we believe the other, he is an advocate of a theism more or less like, if not identical with, Christianity."[113] On the other hand, there is also an interesting synthesis in Aurobindo's mysticism, of the three principal schools of Vedanta-Advaitavada, Visistadvaitavada and Dvaitavada. His integral non-dualism holds that Reality comprises such eternal poises of being of the supreme Spirit as "supra-cosmic transcendence, cosmic universality and unique individuality."[114]

12. Like Aurobindo, Tagore also suggests that the kingdom of Heaven is within us. The thought finds an echo from the holy Upanishadic saying *Tat Tvam Asi* (Thou art That). Salvation is a realization of our Divine Nature—our union with the Divine. Tagore sings, "You were in the centre of my heart, therefore when my heart wandered she never found you, [...]."[115] Aurobindo also points out that the ultimate aim of a gnostic being is to establish the kingdom of God (Divine family) on earth. Following the traditional story of Savitri and Satyavan, Aurobindo makes the legend a symbol of the salvation of man. The return of Savitri and Satyavan to their kingdom is a symbol of the establishment of the kingdom of God on earth through the descent of the Super-Mind.[116]

13. Love in Tagore's mysticism stands for the synthetic principle through which all contraries unite. To him, "love is the highest faculty of the soul. The intellect sets us apart from the things to be known, but love aims at union."[117] When a man is free from the yoke of the little self, egoless universal love emerges which generates in him all-consciousness (*Sarvanubhuti*) Tagore opines that love is the highest bliss that man can attain to, for through it alone he truly knows that he is more than himself, and that he is at one with the All.[118] Further he remarks that Man's "freedom and fulfilment is in love which is another name for perfect comprehension. By this power of comprehension, this permeating of

His being he is united with the all-pervading Spirit, who is also the breath of his soul."[119] This realization is said to be the highest ideal of man. For love is the ultimate meaning of everything around us. It is not a mere sentiment; it is truth; it is the joy that is at the root of all creation.[120] Joy is the revelation of the infinite which is already in us by the light of love that gives the true meaning of our life. And when a man attains the state of *Brahma-vihara,* he sings out of joy:

> The inward and the outward has become as one sky,
> The infinite and the finite are united.
> I am drunken with the sight of this All.[121]

Similarly, Aurobindo thinks that the true divine love leads to the perfect knowledge of the 'Beloved' through perfect intimacy, thus becoming a path of knowledge, and to divine service, thus becoming a path of works. In the same way, perfect knowledge leads to perfect love and joy and a full acceptance of the works of the Supreme; so also dedicated works lead to the love of the Supreme Reality and the deepest knowledge of its ways and being.[122] Further, he marks out that the God-lover is the universal lover and he embraces the All-blissful and All-beautiful. When universal love has seized on his heart it is the decisive sign that the Divine has taken possession of him; and when he has the vision of the All-beautiful everywhere and can feel at all times the bliss of his embrace, that is the decisive sign that he has taken possession of the Divine.[123] The following lines from *Savitri* beautifully sum up the concept of love as propounded by Aurobindo:

> For Love is the bright link twixt earth and heaven,
> Love is the far Transcendent's angel here;
> Love is man's lien on the Absolute [...].[124]

Thus, the noble universalism that permeates the way of life developed and practised by Tagore reaches its zenith in his immaculate conception of Visva-Bharati whose main objects are, first, to realize in a common fellowship of study the meeting of the East and the West, and then ultimately to strengthen the fundamental conditions of world peace through the establishment of free communication of ideas between the two hemispheres. Similarly, for Aurobindo, the realization of the Supermind's significance and intention, by a wide-awake union with its Truth-consciousness, is his contribution to spiritual experience. The systematic detailed exposition of this supra-consciousness is his contribution to philosophy and its direct application to the problems of individual and collective living in his Ashram at Pondicherry is his contribution to practical world-work.

REFERENCES

1. Rabindranath Tagore, *Sadhana* (Calcutta: Macmillan Ltd.: 1913), 158.
2. Rabindranath Tagore, *Creative Unity* (Calcutta: Macmillan Ltd.: 1922), 4.
3. Rabindranath Tagore, *The Diary of a Westward Voyage*: Tr. Indu Dutt (Calcutta: Macmillan Ltd.: 1962), 128-129.
4. Rabindranath Tagore, *Personality* (Calcutta: Macmillan Ltd.: 1917), 56-57.
5. Rabindranath Tagore, *Sadhana* (Calcutta: Macmillan Ltd.: 1913), 70.
6. Rabindranath Tagore, *Chitra* (Calcutta: Macmillan Ltd.: 1918), 19.
7. *Ibid.*, 28.
8. *Ibid.*, 44.
9. *Ibid.*, 60.
10. Rabindranath Tagore, *Creative Unity* (Calcutta: Macmillan Ltd.: 1922), 80.
11. Rabindranath Tagore, *Fruit Gathering* (Calcutta: Macmillan Ltd.: 1916), X.
12. Rabindranath Tagore, *The Religion of Man* (Calcutta: Macmillan Ltd.: 1932), 91.
13. Rabindranath Tagore, *Chitra* (Calcutta: Macmillan Ltd.: 1918), 65-66.
14. Rabindranath Tagore, *Sadhana* (Calcutta: Macmillan Ltd.: 1913), 28.
15. *Ibid.*, 32.
16. *Ibid.*, 54.
17. *Ibid.*, 116.
18. Rabindranath Tagore, *Personality* (Calcutta: Macmillan Ltd.: 1917), 71.
19. K.D. Sethna, *The Poetic Genius of Sri Aurobindo* (Pondicherry: Sri Aurobindo Ashram: 1947), 156.
20. Sri Aurobindo Ghose, *The Life Divine* (Pondicherry: Sri Aurobindo Ashram: 1940), II, 513.
21. R.K. Singh, *Savitri: A Spiritual Epic* (Barielly: Prakash Book Depot: 1984), 153.
22. S. Radhakrishnan, *The Principal Upanishads* (New Delhi: Harper Collins Publishers India Private Ltd.: 1999), 571.

23. Sri Aurobindo Ghose, *The Life Divine* (Pondicherry: Sri Aurobindo Ashram: 1940), 75.
24. S. Radhakrishnan, *The Principal Upanishads* (New Delhi: Harper Collins Publishers India Private Ltd.: 1999), 748.
25. Sri Aurobindo, *Savitri: A Legend and a Symbol* (Pondicherry: Sri Aurobindo Ashram: 1988) Book I: Canto IV: 67.
26. *Ibid.*, 67.
27. Sri Aurobindo, *Savitri: A Legend and a Symbol: op. cit.*, Book I: Canto IV: 63.
28. *Ibid.*, 66.
29. *Ibid.*, 61.
30. Kishore S. Dave, *Upanishad Navneet*: (Ahmedabad: University Grant Nirman Board: 1998).
31. Sri Aurobindo, *Savitri: A Legend and a Symbol: op. cit.*, Book IV: Canto II: 454.
32. S. Radhakrishnan. *The Principal Upanishads: op. cit.*, 557.
33. D.S. Mishra, *Poetry and Philosophy in Sri Aurobindo's Savitri* (New Delhi: Harman Publishing House: 1989), 119.
34. Sri Aurobindo Ghose, *The Life Divine: op. cit.*, 711.
35. *Simon and Schuster Encyclopedia* (CD).
36. *Ibid.*
37. *Ibid.*
38. *Ibid.*
39. Sri Aurobindo, *Savitri: A Legend and a Symbol: op. cit.*, Book X: Canto I: 600-01.
40. *Simon and Schuster Encyclopedia* (CD).
41. S. Radhakrishnan, *The Principal Upanishads: op. cit.*, 632.
42. Swami Chidbhavananda, *The Bhagavat Gita* (Tirupparaitturai: Sri Ramakrishna Tapovanam: 1983), Sloka, 47, 33.
43. Sri Aurobindo, *Essays on the Gita* (Pondicheny: Sri Aurobindo Ashram: 1922), Vol. I.
44. *Simon and Schuster Encyclopedia* (CD).
45. *Ibid.* Canto II: 478.
46. Sri Aurobindo, *Savitri: A Legend and a Symbol: op. cit.*, Book VII: Canto V: 525-26.
47. Rabindranath Tagore, *Personality* (Calcutta: Macmillan Ltd.: 1917), 68-69.
48. Sri Aurobindo, *Savitri: A Legend and a Symbol: op. cit.*, Book VII: Canto II: 486-87.
49. S. Radhakrishnan, *The Principal Upanishads: op. cit.*, 599-607.
50. Mangesh Nadkarni, *Savitri: A Brief Introduction* (Pondicherry: Sri Aurobindo Ashram: 1990), 14-15.

51. *Simon and Schuster Encyclopedia* (CD).
52. Sri Aurobindo, *Savitri: A Legend and a Symbol*: *op. cit.*, (Book VII: Canto I), 465.
53. *Simon and Schuster Encyclopedia* (CD).
54. Sri Aurobindo, *Savitri: A Legend and a Symbol*: *op. cit.*, (Book VI: Canto I), 435.
55. Mangesh Nadkarni, *Savitri: A Brief Introduction* (Pondicherry: Sri Aurobindo Ashram: 1990), 17.
56. K.P.S.Choudhary, *Modern Indian Mysticism* (Delhi: Motilal Banarsidas: 1981), 176.
57. *Ibid.*, l86.
58. *Ibid.*, 229-230.
59. Rabindranath Tagore, *Jivandevata* (11th Feb. 1896).
60. Rabindranath Tagore, *The Diary of a Westward Voyage*: *op. cit.*, 129.
61. Rabindranath Tagore, *Collected Poems and Plays* (Madras: Macmillan India Limited: 1991), 321.
62. K.P.S. Choudhary, *Modern Indian Mysticism* (Delhi: Motilal Banarsidas: 1981), 230.
63. Aurobindo Ghose, *The Life Divine* (Pondicherry: Sri Aurobindo Ashram: 1955), 376.
64. Rabindranath Tagore, *The Diary of a Westward Voyage* (Bombay: Asia Publishing House: 1962), 129.
65. K.P.S. Choudhary, *Modern Indian Mysticism* (Delhi: Motilal Banarsidas: 1981), 230.
66. Rabindranath Tagore: *Sadhana* (London: Macmillan and Company Ltd.: 1926), 164.
67. *Ibid.*, 155.
68. Aurobindo Ghose: *The Life Divine* (Pondicherry: Sri Aurobindo Ashram: 1955), 457.
69. *Ibid.*, 764.
70. *Ibid.*, 122.
71. Rabindranath Tagore, *Sadhana*: *op. cit.*, 159.
72. *Ibid.*, l07.
73. *Ibid.*, 28.
74. *Ibid.*, 107.
75. S. Radhakrishnan, *The Philosophy of Rabindranath Tagore* (Baroda: Good Companions Publishers: 1961), 15.
76. K.P.S. Choudhary, *op. cit.*, 203-204.
77. Rabindranath Tagore, *Sadhana*: *op. cit.*, 10.
78. Rabindranath Tagore, *The Religion of Man* (London: Unwin Books: 1961), 89.

79. Sri Aurobindo, Quoted in *The Visva-Bharati Quarterly*, Vol. 26 (May-July 1951), 17.
80. K.P.S. Choudhary, *op. cit.*, 257.
81. Rabindranath Tagore, *Sadhana*: *op. cit.*, 65.
82. S. Radhakrishnan, *op. cit.*, 59.
83. S.K. Maitra, *The Meeting of the East and the West in Sri Aurobindo's Philosophy* (Pondicherry: Sri Aurobindo Ashram: 1956), 315.
84. Aurobindo Ghose, *The Life Divine*: *op. cit.*, 480.
85. *Ibid.*, 462.
86. *Ibid.*, 480.
87. Aurobindo Ghose, *Savitri: A Legend and a Symbol*: *op. cit.*, 480.
88. K.P.S. Choudhary, *op. cit.*, 204.
89. Rabindranath Tagore, *Sadhana*: *op. cit.*, 32.
90. Rabindranath Tagore, *Man* (London: Macmillan Ltd.: 1959), 11.
91. K.P.S. Choudhary, *op. cit.*, 252.
92. Aurobindo Ghose, *The Life Divine*: *op. cit.*, 1130.
93. Rabindranath Tagore, *Sadhana*: *op. cit.*, 130.
94. Rabindranath Tagore, *The Religion of Man* (London: Macmillan Ltd.: 1961), 112.
95. Rabindranath Tagore, *Sadhana*: *op. cit.*, 130.
96. K.P.S. Choudhary, *op. cit.*, 252.
97. Aurobindo Ghose, *The Life Divine*: *op. cit.*, 1135.
98. Albert Schweitzer, *Indian Thought and Its Development* (Bombay: Wilco Publishing House: 1960), 241.
99. Rabindranath Tagore, *Poems of Kabir* (London: Macmillan and Co. Ltd.: 1961), 3.
100. Rabindranath Tagore, *Gitanjali* (London: Macmillan and Co. Ltd.: 1953) no. 73.
101. Aurobindo Ghose, *The Synthesis of Yoga* (Pondicherry: Sri Aurobindo Ashram: 1957), 10.
102. Aurobindo Ghose, *Bases of Yoga* (Calcutta: Arya Publishing House: 1936), 156.
103. Aurobindo Ghose, *The Synthesis of Yoga*: *op. cit.*, 82.
104. Aurobindo Ghose, *Bases of Yoga*: *op. cit.*, 158-59.
105. Aurobindo Ghose, *The Supramental Manifestation*: (Pondicherry: Sri Aurobindo Ashram: 1952), 42.
106. Rabindranath Tagore, *Sadhana*: *op. cit.*, 32.
107. Aurobindo Ghose, *The Synthesis of Yoga*: *op. cit.*, 945.
108. H. Chaudhuri, *The Philosophy of Integralism* (Calcutta: Sri Aurobindo Pathamandir: 1954), 176.

109. Rabindranath Tagore, *Sadhana*: *op. cit.*, 54.
110. *Ibid.*, 56.
111. Aurobindo Ghose, *Savitri: A Legend and a Symbol*: *op. cit.*, (Book VI, Canto I), 435.
112. R.C. Zaehner, *Hinduism* (London: Oxford University Press: 1962), 247-48.
113. S. Radhakrishnan, *op. cit.*, 2.
114. Aurobindo Ghose, *The Life Divine*: *op. cit.*, 787-88.
115. Rabindranath Tagore, *Fruit Gathering* (Bangalore: Macmillan India Ltd.: 1995), 96.
116. Aurobindo Ghose, *Letters of Sri Aurobindo* (Bombay: Sri Aurobindo Circle: 1950), 36.
117. Rabindranath Tagore. *Sadhana*: *op. cit.*, 159.
118. *Ibid.*, 28.
119. *Ibid.*, 15.
120. *Ibid.*, 107.
121. Rabindranath Tagore, *Personality*: *op. cit.*, 71.
122. Aurobindo Ghose, *The Synthesis of Yoga*: *op. cit.*, 44.
123. *Ibid.*, 675.
124. Aurobindo Ghose, *Savitri: A Legend and a Symbol*: *op. cit.*, 711.

5

Conclusion

Our study of Tagore's *Chitra* and Aurobindo's *Savitri*, in the preceding chapters reveals that both the texts have carved a particular niche for themselves for their thematic concerns, treatment and philosophical depth. Rabindranath Tagore and Aurobindo Ghose drew their inspiration from the *Mahabharata* for their works *viz.*, *Chitra* and *Savitri*, as these heroines of the two works strike a few points of comparison with Gandhari, Kunti, Draupadi, Damyanti, Arundhati, Lopamudra, Sukanya, Odhavati and others. Both Tagore and Aurobindo were thinkers and therefore they have brought about quite a few variations in the original legends of Chitra and Savitri. Tagore and Aurobindo have chosen these stories to fulfil their aesthetic and philosophical purposes. Being good artists they knew very well how to conceal their art. They did not philosophize directly but proposed a mode of self-analysis in order to attain *Vidya* (knowledge). *Chitra* and *Savitri* are works that tell us about the greatest possibilities and purposes of human love and human life.

The impact of the Indian Renaissance, to which Tagore and Aurobindo belong, is clearly discernible in their works. Both appeared on the Indian cultural scene at a time when India was continually experiencing the colonial impact in every sphere of life. Both of them were conscious of the colonial influence generating a habit of mind, which was ever weakening in us the apprehension of truth. In order to rebuild the nation's consciousness it was imperative for the two poets to search for legends that would sink deep into the living texture of a culture, and at the same time would have the widest extension of meaning and signification. This visionary quality of Tagore and Aurobindo created *Chitra* and *Savitri*.

Another significant aspect of *Chitra* and *Savitri* is that they are grounded in the Bengal tradition where women had been subjected to all possible social ordeals as sati-system, child marriage and the refusal to permit widow-remarriage. Tagore and Aurobindo were alive to these social issues and therefore they drew in *Chitra* and *Savitri* women characters who reject these orthodox notions of the contemporary times. The two texts are a record of the progress of the society that Bengal witnessed in matters relating to the position of women in society. They succeeded in injecting the much-needed reformation in the social, cultural and religious position of the women of the times.

The aim of Tagore and Aurobindo was to attain victory over one's false-self and death, in *Chitra* and *Savitri* respectively. The outer world, the society, philosophy, science, art, music reminded them that the ultimate truth in man was in the illumination of the mind, in the extension of consciousness, in the steady evolution of the self, in the recognition of the one Truth, in the recognition for the harmony of contrary forces, in the realization that all things are spiritually one and in acquiring self-knowledge and self-transcendence. Both the writers intended to awaken the self, to raise the life and existence to a higher level of consciousness. Their works showed us how an individual begins with himself, by raising his consciousness, purifying himself and realizing a wider meaning of life. They primarily aimed at the unfolding of the self and the world in their works.

Both the legends of Chitra and Savitri are recreated to recover the human wholeness. They are spiritual in their theme, conception and execution. They believe in the implicit following of one's cultural heritage and familiarity with tradition. In adapting the legends of Chitra and Savitri to contemporary times, both Tagore and Aurobindo were already in an activity of tradition and cultural analysis. The mythical framework of the works highlights the Indian traditions more competently than any other text. The legends have been explored to understand the deepest mysteries of life, love and death and answer some essential existential questions. They depersonalize and become archetypes of the quest theme of the human spirit, which refuses to accept even the limitations of borrowed beauty and death. Thus, the source text—the *Mahabharata*, the impact of the Indian Renaissance on Tagore and Aurobindo, the grounding of the poets in the contemporary Bengal tradition, and the purpose behind the creation of these two works lead us to the reasons behind their choice of the two female characters—Chitra and Savitri.

Generally speaking, the Indian mind is familiar with the idea of God in an eternal feminine aspect and therefore the Indian people have always cherished the legends of the great women of the ancient epics. The Chitra and Savitri legends are suggestive of the commitment that women have towards actualizing their real self and thereby fulfilling the purpose of life. Both of them symbolize the principle of *Shakti,* the creative power that manifests itself in order to fulfil human destiny and the cosmic design of God. The quest of Tagore and Aurobindo is directed towards the realization of human unity, universal peace and happiness. Chitra and Savitri are concerned with the consciousness of men and show how they, like all other living things, grow according to their own nature. They offer to mankind the spectacle of a reawakening and rebirth of spiritual life. Chitra and Savitri extend their consciousness by their experience of life and eventually acquire self-knowledge and self-transcendence. They are educated in the self and in otherness by seeing their self, their other-half, their opposite, their false-selves and finally their whole transcendental being. In *Chitra*, Madana and Vasanta and in *Savitri*, Yoga is the means to enact the ancient story with new motifs. In both the works the action is internal, shifting back and forth on the various planes of consciousness and manifesting a spiritualized uplifting of thought, feeling and sense. The inner mind is the central point, the background of the two mighty opposites—love/beauty, reality/illusion, and love/death, knowledge/ ignorance, of the two works. Both *Chitra* and *Savitri* bear witness to the conscious subjectivity of the modern mind and the expansion of the self. They meditate on the truth of life and the truth of spirit.

Tagore was one of the earliest writers to work on the Chitra episode. The story of *Chitra* revolves around Chitra, a Manipuri princess, who longs to possess Arjuna at all costs. It is a powerful work on the psychological tension of a woman caught between her patience and realization of the importance of physical charm. The most dominant feature of the play, however, is the assertion of equality of women. When Arjuna develops a liking for Chitra, the huntress, Chitra expresses her knowledge of male psyche and reveals the social discrimination in our society. She asks Arjuna in sarcasm whether a woman was merely a woman when she wound herself round men's hearts with her smiles, sobs, services and caressing endearments or when a woman exhibited her learning and achievement. This question of Chitra is very significant as it throws light on our social attitudes towards women. It is taken for granted that a woman is supposed to take care of the man and her primary duty is to entertain him. A man's responsibilities as such do not ever equal that of a woman. The man may do whatever he desires to do. Neither is he supposed to take care of a woman's emotions and nor does he hold dependability in the rearing up of a child. The woman has to behave according to his whims and prejudices. The Man may however, behave according to his likes and dislikes. Moreover, the man has a tendency of not being very appreciative of a woman's accomplishments apart from the wealth of her physical details. The query that Chitra puts forward revolves around the following ideas:

1. Can a man accept a woman devoid of physical beauty without complaint?
2. Is it necessary only for the woman to deck herself and wait on the man?
3. Is it only for the man to satisfy himself without taking into account the wishes of the woman?
4. Is it only for the man to attend to work outside the house?
5. Is it only left for the woman (when she grows old) to be confined to a corner of the house?
6. Cannot the man and the woman share a common footing in terms of caring and working for the house?

Quintessentially, the female-self of Chitra is representative of the everyday issues of the Indian women in general. The debate of man/woman's equality would become perpetual if both were not to value each other. And Arjuna does respond positively to her queries. He does understand the need to recognize a woman's identity/individuality or else the woman would remain a mystery for the man. Chitra and Arjuna's realization is an acknowledgement of each other's individuality. That each one of them reserves the limited space defined for her/him; that no character stands to be marginalized and that each one holds a defined center, forms the pivotal idea of *Chitra.*

On the other hand, Aurobindo was the first to elevate the Savitri episode to epical heights. In *Savitri,* the story rotates around Savitri, a Madri princess who eventually gets married to Satyavan. But he is destined to die within an year. Savitri, inspite of her mental anguish, resolutely decides to confront Death and break the cosmic law of *Karma.* In her quest of the Ultimate, she does not compromise with the laws of Ignorance, Darkness and Death. Rather, she successfully persuades the god of Death to give back the life of the young prince. Savitri's debate with death and her ultimate triumph over mortality have sunk deep into the soul of India (The discussion that ensues between Savitri and Yama holds a similarity with the dialogue that takes place in the *Katha Upanishad* between Nachiketa and Yama).

In *Chitra,* Chitra had a desire in the past to fight a combat with Arjuna and defeat him in it. It obviously points to the concept of equality between man and woman. Chitra believes that both man and woman possess the same quality of intelligence and skill in every deed. And given an opportunity she is capable of proving herself in every sphere of life. *Chitra* consequently marks out the equality between man and woman from the physical and mental points of view. *Savitri* also exhibits the fact that not only holy men—*rishis*—can dare encounter and defy the mighty god of Death, but a woman too, armed with the qualities of *Shakti* (power) and *Bhakti* (devotion), can defeat the god of Death. *Savitri* conclusively indicates the equality between man and woman from the mental and spiritual points of view.

The points of comparison run thus:

1. Both, Chitra and Savitri, are the only children of their parents. They carry a background story of divine birth.

They come from royal respectable families which give them freedom to think, decide and execute deeds according to their wish and will.

2. Both Chitra and Savitri in choosing Arjuna and Satyavan respectively, go on to exhibit their female right, will-power and confidence. Their decision to select their life partners is essentially a continuation of the tradition established by Shakuntala, Ganga, and Sharmistha.
3. Both are the recipients of Divine Grace. Chitra becomes a perfect beautiful damsel like Shruchavati and Sulabha and Savitri defeats the god of Death like Odhavati.
4. Both encounter barriers in the path of love and finally succeed in winning back their life-mates. Chitra displays growth in understanding and realization, while Savitri exhibits growth in consciousness. They realize their 'self' and embody in themselves the qualities of female psyche and unusual female achievement.
5. Both reject the two negations—the ascetic's denial of life and the sensualist's denial of the spirit.
6. Both are concerned with the welfare of humanity in general. They are not self-centred. Rather both see salvation in depersonalization. Chitra, the huntress comes to the aid of the villagers in times of distress, while Savitri dedicates herself to the cause of uplifting mankind. Both, therefore, stand as milestones in the history of women's free thinking.
7. Both exemplify and justify the meanings inherent in their names *viz.*, Chitra—the beautiful image and Savitri—the image of the Sun god.
8. Both exemplify a life that is a synthesis of tradition and modernity. On the one hand they are fully conscious of their rights and on the other they examine their respective roles of cultural representation.
9. Both assert their individuality and identity in relation to others. Chitra presents her true/false being only because she encounters Arjuna and Savitri transcends the physical categories of existence only because she has Satyavan living/dead by her side.

10. Both are responsible for bringing happiness and bliss to their families; they are seen as good friends of their respective life-mates; they are affectionate, intelligent, self-respected women; they are made up of a *jivan shakti* (life-force)/ female-consciousness that makes them distinguished; and they, as would-be mothers, are complete women.
11. Both are seekers of truth and knowledge. They successfully actualize their potential by manifesting their real self through self-upliftment. Chitra discards her borrowed beauty to face Truth as it is and Savitri defeats death by raising herself to a higher plane of consciousness.
12. Both live life as the precious gift of God. They care for the body as the temple of God and think the soul as the ultimate reality.
13. Both reflect Indian culture, Indian women and the way of living life. They assert women's valuable and meaningful place in society and public life.
14. Both exhibit the magic of *Shakti* (power) and the power of *Prakriti* (nature). They symbolize the evolution of the human love and human soul towards the Ultimate Reality.

The present study reveals the following points of contrast:

1. Chitra and Savitri have a fundamental difference in terms of their familial background, social environment and mental makeup which leads to their having a different aptitude, attitude, ideology and approach to life.
2. Chitra loses her distinct personality, though temporarily, for winning the love of Arjuna, while Savitri neither loses nor gives up her personality for winning the love of Satyavan.
3. Chitra struggles with her inner lower self, while Savitri struggles with the outer lower being.
4. Chitra asks for beauty for herself, while Savitri asks for life for her husband.

5. Chitra is devoid of patience, while Savitri is the very embodiment of patience.
6. Chitra's self revolves around matter, life, knowledge, bliss and consciousness, while Savitri's self revolves around matter, life, mind, knowledge, bliss, consciousness and existence.

In spite of these few points of contrast, the two works primarily discuss female-consciousness—*nari chetna*. *Chitra* and *Savitri* succeed in asserting the supremacy of female discourse over male discourse. Chitra initially persuades the male gods (Madana and Vasanta) to see her point of view and then gets from them the boon desired. The boon is again a medium for Chitra to destabilize Arjuna's patriarchal position and she precisely succeeds in doing that when she observes that Arjuna cannot do without her. And then she reveals her true self. Similarly, Savitri through her dialogue with the male god of Death (Yama) subverts the traditional equations. Her victory in getting back Satyavan, is an effort to establish the superiority of female colloquy over male colloquy. The prime object of these female-centred works lies in seeing the subversion of the male-dominated society, valuing the female-self, recognizing the gender-difference and thereby discerning what may be seen as an Indian mode of feminism.

Tagore and Aurobindo, ceaseless experimenters that they were, were perennially in quest for novelty in their creative works. They tended to seek new things by adapting the old legends to present times. The women characters in the *Mahabharata* are powerful but none display the fearless attitude to meeting the challenges of life and death. In the entire gamut of Indian literature only Chitra and Savitri stand apart, as the very models of female will, female psyche and female consciousness. Furthermore, Tagore and Aurobindo have used Chitra and Savitri as symbols of *Saundarya* (beauty) and *Shakti* (power). They are women who can fight even against the greatest of evils—'Illusion' and 'Ignorance' respectively. Their acceptance even in our present times is an indication of the universal appeal that the works evoke irrespective of time and place. They stand as immortal characters, for they ooze with life and ceaseless vitality. Tagore and Aurobindo wanted to guide and shape the contemporary Indian sensibility.

Both Chitra and Savitri guide the contemporary women how to live life, how to be fearless and determined for self-realization.

Conclusively, the *Mahabharata,* the source text of *Chitra* and *Savitri,* reflects the socio-cultural, religious, political and economic conditions of the age. *Chitra* and *Savitri* are certainly the renderings of the ancient Hindu legends and bear close affinities with the mode of the *Vedas* and the *Upanishads.* The concept of ever-increasing inwardness is realized to its full potential in *Chitra* and *Savitri.* Chitra and Savitri gained fame on account of their perseverance in self-analysis and the ultimate realization of their real selves. Tagore and Aurobindo have succeeded to good measure in their endeavour of awakening and fulfilling human-hood in *Chitra* and *Savitri.* Chitra and Savitri are epitomes of the *dharma* of life-force. Thus, Tagore and Aurobindo through *Chitra* and *Savitri* display an uncommon competence and artistic skill in arranging and moulding the legends to suit their literary, social, and philosophical intents and therein lies the secret of their greatness as writers.

Bibliography

PRIMARY SOURCES

Books

Tagore, Rabindranath. *Sadhana*. Calcutta: Macmillan India Limited, 1913.

——. *Personality*. Calcutta: Macmillan India Limited, 1917.

——. *Creative Unity*. Calcutta: Macmillan India Limited, 1922.

——. *The Religion of Man*. Calcutta: Macmillan India Limited, 1932.

——. *Nationalism*. Calcutta: Macmillan India Limited, 1950.

——. *Man*. London: Macmillan Limited, 1959.

——. *The Diary of a Westward Voyage*. Trans. by Indu Dutt, Calcutta: Macmillan Limited, 1962.

——. *Lectures and Addresses*. Madras: Macmillan India, 1970.

——. *Reminiscences*. Madras: Macmillan India Limited, 1971.

——. *The Religion of an Artist*. Calcutta: Viswa-Bharati, 1971.

——. *Poems of Kabir*. Madras: Macmillan India Limited, 1972.

——. *Collected Poems and Plays*. Madras: Macmillan India Limited. 1991.

——. *Chitra*. Delhi: Macmillan India Limited, 1995.

——. *My Boyhood Days*. Calcutta: Viswa-Bharati, 1997.

Ghose, Aurobindo. *Essays on the Gita*. Pondicherry: Sri Aurobindo Ashram, 1922.

——. *Bases of Yoga*. Pondicherry: Sri Aurobindo Ashram, 1936.

——. *The Life Divine*. Pondicherry: Sri Aurobindo Ashram, 1940.

——. *The Future Poetry*. Pondicherry: Sri Aurobindo Ashram, 1953.

——. *The Supramental Manifestation*. Pondicherry: Sri Aurobindo Ashram, 1957.

——. *The Synthesis of Yoga*. Pondicherry: Sri Aurobindo Ashram, 1957.

——. *Eric: A Dramatic Romance*. Pondicherry: Sri Aurobindo Ashram, 1960.

——. *Letters on Poetry, Literature and Art*. Pondicherry: Sri Aurobindo Ashram, 1972.

——. *Isha Upanishad*. Pondicherry: Sri Aurobindo Ashram, 1986.

——. *Savitri. A Legend and a Symbol*. Pondicherry: Sri Aurobindo Ashram, 1988.

SECONDARY SOURCES

Abercrombie, Lascelles. *Principles of Literary Criticism*. Bombay: Vora and Co., Publishers Private Ltd., 1958.

Abrams, M.H. *A Glossary of Literary Terms*. Bangalore: Prism Books Private Limited, 1993.

Aronson, Alex & Kripalani, Krishna. *Rolland and Tagore*. Calcutta: Viswa-Bharati, 1945.

Bhattacharya, Viswanath. *Sanskrit Drama and Dramaturgy*. Varanasi: Bharata Manisha, 1974.

Bhavalkar, Vanmala. *Mahabharat Me Nari*. Sagar: Abhinav Sahitya Prakashan, Samvat 2021.

Chatterji, Sunitikumar. *World Literature and Tagore*. Santiniketan: Viswa-Bharati, 1971.

Chaudhary, Indranath. *Tulanatmak Sahitya Ki Bhumika*. New Delhi: National Publishing House, 1983.

Chaudhuri, H. *The Philosophy of Integralism*. Calcutta: Sri Aurobindo Pathamandir, 1954.

Chattopadhya, Dipankar. *Introduction to Tagore*. Calcutta: Viswa-Bharati, 1988.

Choudhary, K.P.S, *Modern Indian Mysticism*. Delhi: Motilal Banarsidass, 1981.

Das, Bijay Kumar. *Comparative Literature*. New Delhi: Atlantic Publishers and Distributors, 2000.

Das, Manoj. *Sri Aurobindo*. New Delhi: Sahitya Akademi, 1972.

Das, Sisir Kumar. *A History of Indian Literature, 1911-1956.* New Delhi: Sahitya Akademi, 1995.

Dave, Kishore S. *Upanishad Navneet.* Ahmedabad: University Granth Nirman Board-Gujarat Rajya, 1998.

Desai, Jitendra & Vedia Dasharathlal. *Sanskrit Nibandh Parijat.* Ahmedabad: Sanskrit Pustakbhandar, 1970.

Deshpande, R.Y. *Satyavan Must Die.* Bihar: Sri Aurobindo Study Circle, 1996.

Dhavan, R.K (ed.). *Comparative Literature.* New Delhi: Bahri Publications, 1991.

Dikshit, Ratnamayidevi. *Women in Sanskrit Dramas.* Delhi: Meharchand Lachhman Das, 1964.

Ghose, Sisir Kumar. *Rabindranath Tagore.* New Delhi: Sahitya Akademi, 1990.

Ghose, Sisirkumar. *The Poetry of Sri Aurobindo: A Short Survey.* Calcutta: Chatuskone Private Limited, 1969.

Gokak,V.K. *Sri Aurobindo: Seer and Poet.* New Delhi: Abhinav Publications; 1973.

Goodman, W.R. *Quintessence of Literary Essays.* Delhi: Doaba House, 1998.

Gupta, Nolini Kanta. *About Woman.* Trans. Satadal. Pondicherry: Sri Aurobindo Centre for Advanced Research, 1999.

Gupta, Rameshwar. *Eternity in Words.* Bombay: Chetna Prakashan, 1969.

Heehs, Peter. *Sri Aurobindo: A Brief Biography.* Delhi: Oxford University Press, 1993.

Hicks, Rand. *A Savitri Dictionary.* U.S.A.: Integral Knowledge Study Center, 1984.

Hopkins, E. Washburn. *The Great Epic of India: Its Character and Origin.* Calcutta: Punthi Pustak, 1969.

Hudson, William Henry. *An Introduction to the Study of Literature.* New Delhi: Kalyani Publishers, 1979.

Introduction to Tagore. Calcutta: Visva Bharati, 1982.

Iyengar, K.R.S. *Indian Writing in English.* New Delhi: Sterling Publishers Private Limited, 1985.

——. *Sri Aurobindo: An Introduction*. New Delhi: Sterling Publishers Private Limited, 1972.

——. *Dawn to Greater Dawn*. Simla: Indian Institute of Advanced Study, 1975.

Jain, Kunwarlal. *Vedic Sahitya ka Itihas*. Delhi: Bharatiya Vidya Prakashan, 1978.

Jump, John D. *Epic: The Critical Idiom Series*, London: Metheun and Co. Limited, 1971.

Justa, H.R. *Aesthetic Vision of Sri Aurobindo*. Delhi: R.K. Books and Distributors, 1966.

Kalaamani. *Sri Aurobindo: His Mind and Art*. Tricby: Veena Publishers, 1995.

Keith, A.B. *A History of Sanskrit Literature*. London: Oxford University Press, 1966.

Keith, A. Berriedale. *Sanskrit Sahitya ka Itihas*. Trans. by Mangaladev Shastri, Varanasi: Motilal Banarsidass, 1960.

Khshemachandra 'Suman.' *Nari Tere Roop Anek*. Delhi: Atmaram and Sons, 1967.

Kripalani, Krishna. *Rabindranath Tagore: A Biography*. Calcutta: Visva-Bharati, 1980.

Krishna, Shree. *Shreemad Bhagavad Geeta*. Gorakhpur: Govind Bhawan Karyalay, 1943.

Macdonell, A.A. *A History of Sanskrit Literature*. Delhi: Munshi Ram Manohar Lal Oriental Publishers and Booksellers, 1961.

Mahajan, V.D. *History of Medieval India*. New Delhi: S. Chand and Co., 1988.

Maitra, S.K. *The Meeting of the East and the West in Sri Aurobindo's Philosophy*. Pondiherry: Sri Aurobindo Ashram, 1956.

Mehta, Rohit. *The Dialogue with Death*. Calcutta: Motilal Banarsidass Publishers Private Ltd., 1985.

Mishra, D.S. *Poetry and Philosophy in Sri Aurobindo's Savitri*. New Delhi: Herman Publishing House, 1989.

Mukherjee, Prabahat Kumar. *Life of Tagore*. Trans. by Sisir Kumar Ghose, New Delhi: Hind Pocket Books, 1977.

Mulay, D.S. *Ravindranath's Poetry*. Jabalpur: Universal Book Depot, 1964.

Nadkarni, Mangesh. *Savitri: A Brief Introduction*. Pondicherry: Sri Aurobindo Ashram Press, 1990.

Nagendra. (ed.) *Hindi Sahitya ka Itihas*. Allahabad: National Publishing House, 1976.

Naik, M.K. *A History of Indian English Literature*. Bombay: Bharatiya Vidya Bhavan, 1982.

Nandakumar, Prema. *A Study of Savitri*. Pondicherry: All India Books, 1985.

——. *Sri Aurobindo: A Critical Introduction*. Bangalore: Sterling Publishers Private Limited, 1988.

Nandi, Tapasvi. *Sanskrit Natakono Parichay*. Ahmedabad: University Granth Nirman Board—Gujarat Rajya, 1971.

Nicholson, Linda J. *Feminism/Postmodernism*. New York: Routledge, 1990.

Pandeya, Devendranath. *Kathopanishad*. Jaipur: Hansa Prakashan, 1997.

Pandit, M.P. *Yoga in Savitri*. Pondicherry: Dipti Publications, 1995.

——. *Essays on Savitri*: Pondicherry: Sri Aurobindo Ashram, 1969-71.

Paranjape, Makarand. *Indian Poetry in English*. Bangalore: Macmillan India Limited, 1993.

Peck, John & Coyle, Martis. *Literary Terms and Criticism*. London: The Macmillan Press Limited, 1995.

Poddar, S.K. *Sanskrit Sahitya Ka Itihas*. Kashi: Nagari-Pracharini Sabha, Samvat 2011.

Purani, A.B. *Sri Aurobindo's Savitri: An Approach and a Study*. Pondicherry: Sri Aurobindo Ashram, 1970.

Radhakrishnan, S. *The Principal Upanishads*. London: Macmillan and Co., 1953.

——. *Living with a Purpose*. New Delhi: Orient Paperbacks, 1978.

——. *The Philosophy of Rabindranath Tagore*. Baroda: Good Companions Publishers, 1961.

Raja, C. Kunhan. *Survey of Sanskrit Literature.* Bombay: Bharatiya Vidya Bhavan, 1962.

Ram, Sadhu. *Essays on Sanskrit Literature.* Delhi: Munshi Ram Manohar Lal Oriental Booksellers and Publishers, 1965.

Reddy, V. Madhusudan. *Savitri: Epic of the Eternal.* Hyderabad: Aurodarshan Trust, 1984.

Rees, R.J. *English Literature: An Introduction for Foreign Readers.* Madras: Macmillan Press, 1973.

Sandesara, Upendraray. *Shakuntala Ane Savitri.* Ahmedabad: Gujarat University, 1977.

Sastri, K.S. Ramaswami. *Sir Rabindranath Tagore: His Life. Personality and Genius.* Delhi: Akashdeep Publishing House, 1988.

Schweitzer, Albert. *Indian Thought and Its Development.* Bombay: Wilco Publishing House, 1960.

Sethna, K.D. *Aspects of Sri Aurobindo.* U.S.A.: The Integral Life Foundation, 1995.

——. *Sri Aurobindo—The Poet.* Pondicherry: Sri Aurobindo Ashram, 1970.

——. *The Poetic Genius of Sri Aurobindo.* Pondicherry: Sri Aurobindo Ashram, 1947.

Seturaman, V.S. *Indian Aesthetics—An Introduction.* Madras: Macmillan India Limited, 1992.

Shastri, Shakuntala Rao. *Women in the Vedic Age.* Ed. K.M. Munshi and N.C. Aiyer, Bombay: Bharatiya Vidya Bhavan, 1954.

Simon and Schuster Encyclopedia (CD).

Singh, Bacchan. *Aadhunik Hindi Sahitya Ka Itihas.* Allahabad: Lokbharti Prakashan, 1977.

Singh, R.K. *Savitri: A Spiritual Epic.* Bareilly: Prakash Book Depot, 1984.

Skyes, Marjorie. *The Story of Rabindranath Tagore.* Patna: Orient Longman, 1976.

Srivastava, Ramesh K. *Symbolism in Indian Fiction in English.* Jalandar: ABC Publications, 1997.

Trivedi, Ramesh M. *Arvachin Gujarati Sahitya no Itihas.* Ahmedabad: Adarsh Prakashan, 1993-94.

Tyagi, Prem. *Sri Aurobindo: His Poetry and Poetic Theory.* Saharanpur: Ashir Prakashan, 1988.

Vedvyas, Maharshi. *Shri Mahabharata.* Trans. by Pandit Ramnarayan Dutt Shastri Pandeya, Gorakhpur: Geeta Press, Samvat 2045.

Warden, A.K. *Indian Kavya Literature.* Delhi: Motilal Banarsidass, 1972.

Winternitz, Maurice. *A History of Indian Literature.* Delhi: Motilal Banarsidass, 1996.

Wollstonecraft, Mary. *The Rights of Woman.* London: Phoenix Orion Books Limited, 1996.

Zaehner, R.C. *Hinduism.* London: Oxford University Press, 1962.

Articles

Ghose, Sisir Kumar. "Sri Aurobindo's Gita," *Influence of Bhagwadgita on Literature Written in English: in Honour of Ramesh Mohan.* Ed. R.T. Sharma, Meerut, India: Shalabh, 1988.

Harish, Ranjana. "In the Cultural Hall of Mirrors: Issue of Gender Genre Incompatibility of Women's Autobiography." *The Literary Criterion.* 1996.

Sarkar, Ranjit. "Rabindranath Tagore: From Romanticism to Modernism," *Mother India.* Ed. K.D. Sethna. Pondicherry: Sri Aurobindo Ashram Trust Publication Department, July 2000.

Shah, Anil. "Naarinu Aatmagaurav," *Parab.* October 2000.

Singh Shahi, S.M.P.N. "Aurobindo's Savitri: A Cosmic Epic," *The Quest.* Ed. Ravi Nandan Sinha, Ranchi: Sonal Publisher, December 1998.

Singh, A.K., "De/Re-Constructing Kalidasa's *The Abhigyan-shakuntalam.*" *Critical Practice.* Vol. VI, No. 2. Delhi: Creative Books, June 1999.

——. "Bhartendu Harishchandra Aur Bhartiya Navajagran." *Bhartiya Navajagaran Aur Bhartendu Tatha Narmad Yugin Sahitya.* Ed. Mahavirsingh Chauhan. Ahmedabad: Parsh Prakashan, 1996.

Singh, R.K. "Savitri: Sri Aurobindo's Spiritual Romance," *University News*. February 7, 1994.

Thanki, Jyotiben. "Sri Arvindani Advitiya Kruti—Savitri," *Akhand Anand*. August 2000.

INDEX